356
SuL

DATE DUE

FEB 11 1997		
APR 27 1998		
NOV 12 1999		
JA 10 '03		
MR 07 '03		
OC 22 '03		
OC 05 '05		
MR 08 '06		
AP 23 '07		
SEP 25 '07		
MAY 15 '08		
NOV 18 '10		

FOLLETT

Elite Warriors

Elite Warriors

★ THE SPECIAL FORCES OF THE UNITED STATES AND ITS ALLIES

George Sullivan

 Facts On File®

AN INFOBASE HOLDINGS COMPANY

Elite Warriors: The Special Forces of the United States and Its Allies

Copyright © 1995 by George Sullivan

Facts On File, Inc.
460 Park Avenue South
New York NY 10016

Library of Congress Cataloging-in-Publication Data

Sullivan, George, 1927–
Elite Warriors : the special forces of the United States and its
allies / George Sullivan
p. cm.
Includes bibliographical references and index.
Summary: Examines the training and operation of the specialized military units in the armed services of the United States and some of its allies.
ISBN 0-8160-3110-X
1. Special forces (Military science)–United States–Juvenile
literature. 2. Special forces (Military science)–Juvenile
literature. [1. Special forces (Military science)] I. Title.
U262.S95 1995
356′.16–dc20 94-41247

Facts On File books are available at special discounts when purchased in bulk quantities for businesses, associations, institutions or sales promotions. Please call our Special Sales Department in New York at 212/683-2244 or 800/322-8755.

Text design by Catherine Rincon Hyman
Jacket design by Steve Brower

This book is printed on acid-free paper.

Printed in the United States of America

RRD FOF 10 9 8 7 6 5 4 3 2 1

Contents

Sergeant John Moran, as a member of the U.S. Army's 7th Special Forces Group (Airborne), combines the skills of a paratrooper, ranger, and teacher.
(Wide World)

Introduction

A few minutes before 1:00 A.M. on December 20, 1989, U.S. military forces launched their biggest military campaign since the Vietnam War, Operation Just Cause, the invasion of Panama. Some 4,000 Special Operations commandos—popularly known as the Green Berets—provided most of the punch, seizing key objectives. Troopers representing Delta Force, the nation's foremost counterterrorist unit, rescued a jailed American and pursued General Manuel Noriega, Panama's most powerful leader. Navy SEALs—*SE*a, *A*ir, *L*and commandos—destroyed Noriega's boats and planes. Air Force Special Operations personnel in AC-130 Spectre gunships supported U.S. ground troops and destroyed enemy command and control facilities. Airborne Rangers were assigned to seize three key airfields—and did.

The Green Berets, Delta Force, the Army's Rangers, the Navy's SEALs, and the Air Force's special-ops air units—these are the Special Operations forces of the United States, the nation's "secret warriors."

Special Operations commandos are the military's toughest, best-trained, best-equipped soldiers. They are the men who take on the high-risk missions that demand quick and decisive results. They played a vital role in the Persian Gulf War in 1991 and 1992: One military expert called them "the brains behind the brawn in Desert Storm." U.S. Special Forces also led the way in 1993 and 1994 in Operation Restore Hope, the effort to deliver food to the people of famine-stricken Somalia.

A member of the Army's Rangers holds up a pair of AK-47s captured during an attack on a unit of the Panamanian Defense Force during the invasion of Panama in 1989. *(Wide World)*

Today, the U.S. military includes almost 50,000 members of Special Operations forces. They are often secretive soldiers, working in small fighting groups, using exotic weapons and equipment. Able to move quickly to any part of the globe, they are trained to strike by land, sea, or air under all conditions.

Operating behind enemy lines, Special Forces also organize, train, and direct foreign troops in guerrilla warfare tactics. They are trained in survival techniques, languages, communications, weapons, and explosives.

The Army represents the biggest slice of the Special Forces Command, with about 30,000 members. These are the men who make up the famed Green Berets, the Rangers (the Army's elite assault team), and Delta Force, the supersecret unit that deals in counterterrorist operations.

The SEALs are the Navy's contribution to the Special Operations Command. Specializing in amphibious commando raids, the SEALs and their support staff number about 5,500. This includes Team-6, the SEALs' antiterrorist team.

The Air Force's portion of the Special Operations Command includes some 11,000 air commandos. Their job is to provide the helicopters, transport planes, gunships, electronic warfare aircraft, and any other type of aerial support required by the commando units.

As for the U.S. Marine Corps, made up of almost 200,000 men and women, it ranks as the world's largest elite force. The Marines took part in all major operations during the Vietnam War, suffering more than 100,000 casualties. More recently, they were called upon when the United States invaded Grenada and Panama and during the Persian Gulf War. The Marine Corps, however, is a separate branch of the U.S. Armed Forces and is not included in the U.S. Special Operations Command.

Almost all major military powers have specialized military units, not just the United States. The oldest unit is Great Britain's Special Air Service, which came into existence during World War II. Israel has promoted the concept of special military units since the day the nation was founded in 1948. Its elite infantry, paratroop, and armored units, assigned the most difficult military tasks, have won legendary fame throughout the world.

Not long before dawn on September 5, 1972, a band of Arab terrorists scaled a six-foot-high wire fence that surrounded the Olympic Village in Munich, Germany, and went

Special Forces personnel are trained to strike by land, sea, or air. Here Green Berets from Fort Bragg, North Carolina, practice parachuting skills.
(Wide World)

on a rampage, killing 11 Israeli athletes. The murders horrified the world and helped to spur several nations to create special military units to combat terrorists and rescue hostages. In Germany, GSG9 (Grenzschutzgruppe 9) was established as a special unit of the nation's border guard. France set up the GIGN (Group D'Intervention de la Gendarmerie Nationale) as a counterterrorist unit. Today, virtually every fighting force of any size in the world has its elite troops.

In the United States, the concept of Special Operation forces is directly linked to World War II and the efforts of Major General William J. "Wild Bill" Donovan, founder of the OSS, the Office of Strategic Services. Donovan's organization, described as a "new instrument of war" by the U.S. Special Operations Command, was responsible for guerrilla operations, unconventional warfare, intelligence, and counterintelligence during the war. In recognition of Donovan's contribution, the U.S. Special Operations Command adopted as its emblem the gold spearhead on a black background that General Donovan had created for the OSS half a century before.

U.S. Special Forces operations have not always been successful. Far from it, in fact. A raid to rescue the American merchant ship *Mayaguez* and its 34-man crew, seized by Cambodian forces in the Gulf of Siam in 1975, went awry because of poor planning by the Defense Department. In 1980, a Delta Force mission to free 53 Americans held hostage in the U.S. Embassy in Teheran ended in disaster when a Navy helicopter and an Air Force transport plane collided at a remote desert airstrip in Iran. Eight American servicemen died, and no hostages were rescued. In the 1983 invasion of the island of Grenada, a dozen commandos representing Special Operations units were killed or wounded in failed missions.

Disturbed by these failures, Congress ordered the Department of Defense to establish an umbrella operation that would bring all Special Forces under one authority. The U.S. Special Operations Command, with headquarters at MacDill Air Force Base near Tampa, Florida, was the result. It became a reality on June 1, 1987.

Special Forces missions often involve infiltration. Here a Special Forces soldier from Fort Bragg, North Carolina, appears in desert dress, preparing for a role as a "friendly sheik."
(Wide World)

General James J. Lindsay, who had headed a Green Berets team in Vietnam and was decorated for valor and bravery several times, became the first commander of the new organization. Lindsay was succeeded by General Carl Stiner in 1990. A Vietnam veteran who was wounded in action, Stiner has been described as the "best fast-attack general in the U.S. Army." His daring night invasion of Panama, using mostly Special Forces units, although not mistake free, was successful enough to restore some of the luster to the reputation of American commandos. In May 1993, General Wayne A. Downing took over as head of the U.S. Special Operations Command from General Stiner. General Downing had commanded a Special Operations task force during the Persian Gulf War.

More than a few military experts see the Special Forces as the wave of the future. When the Cold War ended and the Soviet Union collapsed in late 1991, it signaled new and leaner days for America's armed forces. Military spending was slashed. Troop levels dropped. The Army and Navy had to learn to make do with fewer but more-versatile weapons. Yet the armed forces still have to be fully equipped and highly mobile, ready to respond to a crisis anywhere in the world. What's needed is a quick-reaction force. The Special Forces meet that need. Many military experts believe the Special Forces will play a critical role in fighting tomorrow's wars.

A gold spearhead on a black background is the insignia of the U.S. Special Forces Command.
(U.S. Special Forces Command)

In May 1993, General Wayne A. Downing was named to head the U.S. Special Operations Command.
(U.S. Special Operations Command)

His face covered with camouflage makeup, a Special Forces soldier creeps through thick jungle underbrush during training exercises in Puerto Rico. *(Wide World)*

U.S. ARMY SPECIAL FORCES

"People have the impression that all we do is run around and blow things up with knives in our teeth," says General Carl Stiner, who once headed the U.S. Special Operations Command. "It isn't that way. These guys can do anything."

Stiner is speaking, of course, about the Army's Special Forces, popularly known as the Green Berets. To some they are Rambos, weirdos and "snake-eaters," soldiers who thrive on personal glory. But the truth is that Green Berets, while individualistic, are trained to be team-minded. And while they are capable of striking deep within enemy territory to blow up bridges or wipe out concentrations of enemy troops, their main job is to help foreign governments train forces that can oppose enemy guerrillas or other rebel groups. To carry out that assignment, they have to be prepared to "do anything." In the Persian Gulf War, doing anything included helping Kurdish refugees and treating injured animals at the Kuwait City zoo.

As of the early 1990s, no more than 5,000 men had the right to wear the green beret and the small crescent-shaped shoulder patch that says SPECIAL FORCES, and to serve with one of the Special Forces' units. The beret and the shoulder patch identify the only "real" Green Berets. There are other men and some women in Special Forces units, generally support personnel such as gate-guards and office workers, who are permitted to wear the beret. But only the true Special Forces soldier gets to wear the Special Forces patch on his shoulder. The others can't be assigned overseas, nor can they be part of a Special Forces team.

Everything is based on the team, the "Operational Detachment/Alpha," or A-team. Nowadays, the team is normally made up of 11 carefully trained and chosen soldiers, plus the captain who commands them. Second in command is a warrant officer, an officer who has been promoted from the enlisted ranks. There is a team sergeant, two weapons specialists, two medical corpsmen, two communications experts, two engineers, and a specialist in intelligence work.

Of course, the team doesn't absolutely have to have 12 members. The number will vary with the mission and the personnel that happen to be available. In the Persian Gulf War, teams composed of six men were secretly helicoptered into Iraq to scoop up soil samples to take back to their headquarters. They also photographed the terrain with camcorders and still cameras. The soil samples were needed to assure that the ground would be firm enough for Allied tanks and trucks, and the videotape and film the teams brought back gave commanders an advance picture of the battlefield.

For administrative purposes, 10 A-teams are formed into a company. Three companies combine with a headquarters unit to form a battalion. It is the battalion that is the team's lifeline, providing supplies and communications support.

Each battalion is part of a group. As of the early 1990s, there were eight groups: the 1st, 5th, 7th, and 10th were on active duty; the 11th and 12th were part of the U.S. Army Reserve; and the 19th and 20th were National Guard groups. Each group has three Special Forces battalions.

Groups and battalions specialize in operating in specific geographical areas. A group might be assigned to Central America, for instance. In such a case, anyone assigned to the group would spend a good deal of time studying the languages and culture of the area.

So much for structure and organization. What, exactly, do Special Forces soldiers do?

Unconventional warfare, or simply UW, is their chief mission. The word "unconventional" means "uncommon or unusual." Unconventional warfare means going behind the lines (which is certainly uncommon or unusual) to organize, equip, train, and lead people who want to resist the enemy from within. It's the basic mission that the founders of the Special Forces had in mind when they first brought the organization into existence during the early 1950s.

In the early days of the Persian Gulf crisis in 1990, the U.S. Special Operations Command proposed a typical unconventional warfare mission for the Green Berets. It was suggested that teams be helicoptered into Iraq to stir up resistance to Saddam Hussein, the Iraqi leader. The plan was rejected, however, because it was feared that if the Green Berets were discovered and their mission revealed, that might accidentally start a war. American policymakers shuddered at such a thought.

A common form of unconventional warfare is guerrilla warfare. A guerrilla is a member of a small, roving band of fighting men who harass the enemy with ambushes and sudden raids. Guerrilla warfare is hit-and-run warfare. It involves operations that are conducted with surprise and carried out with great speed and mobility.

The Special Forces' missions are sometimes strategic reconnaissance missions, or spy missions. A team or teams will be sent into enemy territory to gather intelligence, destroy a strategic target, or recover prisoners.

In the Persian Gulf War, the Green Berets carried out a critical strategic reconnaissance mission. More than a dozen Special Forces A-teams were helicoptered into southern Iraq in the days before the ground war began (on January 17, 1991). They spent their first hours in enemy territory digging holes in the desert sand to use as "hide sites," reinforcing them with slabs of prefabricated material. (The Green Berets in Iraq adopted some of the hide-site techniques they had learned from the Vietcong during the war in Vietnam.)

From their hiding places, the Green Berets used periscopes to watch for any movement on the part of the Iraqi Army. Battlefield commanders wanted to be assured that the Iraqis were not preparing to counterattack from the north, a move that could put in jeopardy a bold flanking maneuver planned by the Allies. Thanks to the coded radio messages the Green Berets sent back to their headquarters, Allied forces were never caught off guard.

Green Berets also took part in strike missions in Iraq. Strike missions are usually used against a strategic target such as an airstrip, a communications center, or perhaps a key piece of terrain.

In Iraq during the Persian Gulf War, the Green Berets attacked enemy command posts and sabotaged lines of communication. One eight-man team, trapped deep in Iraq, was attacked by some 150 enemy soldiers. It managed to fight them off for more than six hours. By the time it was finally rescued by helicopter, the team had killed 130 of the enemy.

Of course, not every mission conducted by the Green Berets gets to be so violent, so deadly. Much more common than the strategic reconnaissance missions and strike missions of the Persian Gulf War are foreign internal defense missions, called FID missions for short. When assigned to a FID mission, Green Berets work with a friendly government in training officers to use their regular forces to defeat guerrillas or any instance of lawlessness or subversion. During the 1980s, dozens of nations called upon the United States to lend such assistance.

No matter what type of mission members of the Special Forces are ultimately assigned, all undergo the same program of instruction and training. It is called the Q (for "qualification") course. It is given in a green, hilly, and remote region of central North Carolina about 35 miles northwest of Fort Bragg.

Undoubtedly, there are many thousands of soldiers who would like to become Green Berets, but only a small handful are able to qualify for the Q course. To become a Green Beret, the Army says you must be "mature and motivated, and open

Members of a Special Forces unit leave the water after a scuba-diving and safety training session conducted by SEAL instructors.
(Wide World)

and humble, particularly with other races and cultures." You must be able "to display independence and authority." You must be "innovative and a team player."

These characteristics are hard to measure, but other qualities that candidates must have aren't. You must be a male soldier, have a high school diploma and score well on special written tests, have become airborne-qualified by completing the parachute-training course at Fort Benning, Georgia, have been granted security clearance, and have at least 21 months remaining on your enlistment.

Those who qualify must, at times, be sorry they did. Everything about the Q course is tough. It lasts 16 to 25 weeks, depending on one's specialty. Trainees arrive in buses in groups of 200. They're made to line up in formation and then run to the school compound, which is about a mile and a half away, carrying their gear. Some can't do it. They've failed the Q course without even having gone through the gate.

Others flunk out on the first day, which offers plenty of push-ups, running, and long marches with a full knapsack.

The buildings at the training compound have seen better days. Most are covered in tar paper and have a Third World look to them. The showers are cold. The meals are nutritious but usually consist of MREs, the Meals-Ready-to-Eat that the Army spent years developing. They're hard to digest and most portions taste like either sugared Styrofoam or salted Styrofoam.

The Q course is divided into three phases, with no days off. The first phase, which lasts 27 days, is very physical. You learn to travel three to five miles at a time with a knapsack on your back. You usually have to cover a mile every 15 minutes, or faster, but at least twice a week the pace is jacked up to a mile every eight minutes, or faster. At the beginning of the first phase, the knapsack weighs 45 pounds; by the end, it's been increased to 65 pounds. There is also a good deal of running without knapsacks. And push-ups; there are always push-ups.

Land navigation training is also part of the first phase. In one test, you're sent into a heavily wooded area and assigned

to find four survey stakes that are about a mile apart. You have five hours to find all four. If you don't find them, you're through. You can be recycled if you want, that is, start again with the next class.

The survival training exercise, also a part of the first phase, lasts three days. You're sent out into the piney woods with a knife, a poncho, a book of matches, and a live rabbit. "Remember to kill it before you eat it," your grinning instructor is likely to tell you.

Trainees learn rappelling on a tower. (Rappelling is a way of moving down a steep incline by means of a double rope

Rappelling is a vital skill when one is operating in mountainous areas. It's also a way of infiltrating into enemy-occupied areas.
(Wide World)

secured above, that is placed around the body and one thigh and paid out gradually.) You learn the techniques to be used in raids and ambushes.

About 50 percent of the trainees flunk out during the first phase. Another 25 to 40 percent are dropped during phase two, which is mostly classroom work. Students are drilled in the specialties they've chosen—engineering, communications, weapons, or medicine. The medical course is given at Fort Sam Houston in Texas, the others at Fort Bragg.

In the third and final phase, trainees take part in simulated UW missions. Local farmers often get into the act, allowing Green Berets to use their farmlands and forests. Some townspeople play the part of helpful guerrillas, driving the Green Berets around in their pickup trucks.

Actually, the Q course is just the beginning of training for Special Forces soldiers. There are additional courses in such subjects as mountaineering, scuba diving, jungle warfare, intelligence analysis, and many others. For the Green Berets, training never really stops.

The story of the Army's Special Forces begins in the 1950s. Colonel Aaron Bank, a veteran of World War II with experience in operating behind the Japanese lines in Southeast Asia, was a key figure in the founding of the organization. Colonel Bank started a school at Fort Bragg, North Carolina, in 1952, to train volunteers "to infiltrate by land, sea, or air deep into enemy-occupied territory and organize the resistance/guerrilla potential to conduct special forces' operations with an emphasis on guerrilla warfare."

Bank looked for volunteers with Ranger or parachute experience during wartime, men who had shown themselves to be reliable and willing to learn new tricks. He also wanted his men to be able to speak a foreign language or two, since they would be operating behind enemy lines.

The men that Bank recruited and trained were divided into eight-man teams. Each team was commanded by a captain and included specialists in communications, weapons, demolition, intelligence-gathering, and medicine. Team members became experts in sabotage, ambush, reconnaissance, and underground resistance.

There are several different versions of the story of how the Special Forces came to wear green berets, but they all agree on one point: President John F. Kennedy was a vital factor.

The beret was common headwear in Germany, France, and many other European countries where Special Forces soldiers were being sent on training missions. It was worn not only by civilians, the soldiers noted, but also by British and French commandos and members of the French Foreign Legion. The American soldiers started wearing berets so that they would look like everyone else, so they would fit in.

Who was the first Special Forces soldier among the troops stationed at Fort Bragg to wear a beret? Don Gehb is usually given the credit. Gehb, later a bank president in California, says that he was inspired by a World War II movie about British commandos. After watching the film, Gehb and several other young soldiers went shopping in the women's clothing stores in Fayetteville, near Fort Bragg, where they found not only green berets, but black and red ones, too. Green was their favorite color and they wore green berets at their next training session.

The idea caught on, and soon teams of Special Forces soldiers were wearing berets on missions in the field. But they had to be careful that nobody in authority was looking when they wore them because the beret had no official endorsement. To wear one was to be out of uniform.

It was around this time, in 1960, that John F. Kennedy was elected president. Kennedy was interested in unconventional warfare and fascinated by the Special Forces and their jaunty green berets.

In October 1961, Kennedy was scheduled to visit Fort Bragg to watch the soldiers perform various tactical exercises. "Are the Special Forces in it?" Kennedy asked his military advisor, Major General Chester Clifton. Clifton said he thought they would be.

Don Gehb, who is credited with being the first Special Forces soldier to wear a Green Beret, poses with a commercial version of the headwear.
(Wide World)

Then, just three days before the visit, the president asked again, "Will I see the Special Forces?"

"Yes, Sir," General Clifton answered. "I've been down to Fort Bragg and I've been working on it."

Then the president asked, "Will the Special Forces have green berets on?"

"Well, Mr. President, they don't have green berets now," said General Clifton.

The president was not pleased. He said, "Well, I've exercised the full authority of the presidency to put a green beret on a few troops and it hasn't worked. Now, you know the inside of the Pentagon; you see if we can have those green berets on those troops. These soldiers have this tremendous, tough job, and they need something special."

Three days later, when President Kennedy visited Fort Bragg and met the commanding officer of the Special Forces, General Williams P. Yarborough, the general was wearing a green beret, and so were 800 of his troops.

The president said, "General Yarborough, these are very nice. How do you like the green beret?"

"They're fine," the general replied.

Then the president grinned and asked, "Incidentally, general, how long have you had them?"

"Since the day before yesterday," the general said, "when the Army got word that if we didn't put these on, you weren't coming to Fort Bragg."

President Kennedy did much more than merely influence the type of headwear favored by Special Forces soldiers. Thanks to his interest and support, unconventional warfare became a popular doctrine in the military. Hundreds of Special Forces teams were sent to almost every part of the globe to train foreign military units in battling Communists.

President Kennedy's contribution has not been forgotten. After the president's assassination in November 1963, the Green Berets renamed their Fort Bragg training school the John F. Kennedy Special Warfare Center.

Special Forces troops went on active duty in the late 1950s and early 1960s. At the time, the United States and its democratic allies were engaged in the Cold War with the Soviet Union and other Communist nations. It was typified by decades of intense rivalry, suspicion, and distrust. But the hostility always stopped short of a shooting war, a "hot" war.

A turning point in the Cold War came in 1950, when North Korean troops invaded South Korea and the Korean War began. U.S. forces went to the aid of South Korea. Bloody fighting continued until 1953, when an armistice was signed.

With the Korean War, the United States had expanded its opposition to Communism into the Far East. Then came Vietnam.

During the early 1960s, the United States began sending men, equipment, and supplies to Vietnam in support of the South Vietnamese in their struggle against the Communist Vietcong. At first, the idea was to help the South Vietnamese to defend themselves, rather than to do the fighting for them. American servicemen and women in Vietnam were called "advisors." They sought to train South Vietnamese soldiers in the use of weapons and tactics, while seeking to instill in them a sense of teamwork and dedication.

The Green Berets were included in this mission in 1961, beginning with a program called the Civilian Irregular Defense Group. The program was based in the Central Highlands of Vietnam and involved the primitive tribesmen who lived there known as the Montagnards, or mountaineers. The Montagnards were hunters and farmers who occupied small towns and villages with strange-sounding names—Bon Sar Pa, Cheo Reo, Ban Me Thout, and Boun Enao. The men hunted with crossbows and spears and wore loincloths, and the women wore skirts of woven cotton. The tribes had been easily conquered by Vietcong invaders from the north.

Late in 1961, eight Special Forces troopers were helicoptered into the Central Highlands to establish a camp in the tiny village of Boun Enao. It was an area wholly dominated by the

Vietcong, who had shut down the local government and ruled with an iron hand, forcing the people to grow rice for them.

When the people of Boun Enao learned that the small band of Green Berets was there to help them fight the Vietcong, they were thrilled. The men lined up eagerly to receive the weapons and ammunition the Green Berets handed out, and the tribesmen willingly began training.

A Special Forces soldier plans strategy with Montagnard tribesmen at Pleimrong in the Central Highlands of Vietnam in 1962.
(Wide World)

Boun Enao was the first camp of its kind established by the Green Berets. Within a year, there were 200 others that involved some 12,000 tribesmen.

Teams made up of several Green Berets and nine or ten tribesmen often took part in patrol missions through the thick jungles of the Central Highlands. The patrols would do reconnaissance, capture prisoners for interrogation, or mine the trails used by the trucks that kept the enemy in food and supplies.

A patrol normally lasted five or six days. The team leader, usually an American, planned the mission, rehearsed the team members, and made arrangements as to when and where the team was to be deployed by helicopter.

Once on the ground, the team waited and listened. If there were enemy soldiers in the area and members of the team could hear them coming, they would instantly radio the helicopter and be airlifted out. But if it was quiet and there were no enemy soldiers nearby, the team would move out, trudging single file, led by a "point man," with a "tail gunner" at the rear.

Patrols moved slowly, for much of the time was spent listening for the enemy. A team would move forward for 20 or so minutes, then halt to listen for 10 minutes. Sometimes it would take a full day to move a couple of miles.

Team members were instructed to avoid overconfidence, which could lead to carelessness. A handbook for those going on patrol advised: "Just because you haven't seen the enemy for three or four days doesn't mean he isn't there and hasn't seen you. You are never 100 percent safe until you are back home."

Just before darkness fell, the team would establish a safe location to sleep, called a "RON," a "remain overnight" position. It was not unusual for patrols to be followed by the enemy, who watched and waited for a chance to attack, so the RON had to be chosen with great care. If discovered by the enemy, the RON invited an ambush.

The team leader would choose a location for the RON, then move a few hundred yards beyond it and select a second

A member of the
Green Berets
helps Montagnard
troops build a
bunker in
Kontrum in the
Central Highlands
of Vietnam.
(Wide World)

location. The team would begin making preparations to spend the night in the first location. But once it was dark, the team would pack up and shift to the second site. Team members would place antipersonnel mines around the site's perimeter, set up defensive positions to be used if an attack came, then eat and try to sleep.

Mining trails used at night by the enemy to move supplies was risky business. Most trails were heavily guarded by the enemy. While members of the team watched a trail from both directions, the team's engineer would use his K-bar knife to dig a hole in the hard-packed soil, plant the mine, replace the soil, and camouflage the spot with leaves and jungle growth.

At night, while at rest, patrols would sometimes hear the mines they had planted during the day go off, evidence that they had done their job well.

Other missions involved capturing prisoners. One method was to wait by a trail for a column of enemy soldiers to go by. If there happened to be a straggler, two or three members of the team would pounce on the man, disarm him, and drag him into the jungle, where he would be handcuffed and gagged.

Later the prisoner would be questioned. Sometimes a prisoner would reveal where the enemy stored its ammunition or food. Air strikes would then be ordered to destroy the storage areas.

By 1964, approximately 18,000 Montagnards, operating out of fortified villages, had begun to regain control of the Central Highlands. They were also playing an important role in reconnaissance.

That same year, 1964, the Green Berets in Vietnam introduced what they called Studies and Observation Groups (SOG). That was the innocent-sounding name for units whose job it was to cross the borders into the neighboring countries of Laos and Cambodia in an effort to pinpoint enemy troop concentrations. The units included U.S. Navy SEALs and U.S. Marine Corps reconnaissance personnel as well as Green Berets.

In 1965, the Green Berets went a step beyond the espionage activities of the SOGs by creating Mobile Strike Force teams to attack Vietcong training camps in Laos and Cambodia. These raids had a high success rate.

Meanwhile, the war had become much more widespread and the United States was sending combat troops to Vietnam in huge numbers. By 1968, more than half a million U.S. troops were fighting in Vietnam in what was to become the fourth bloodiest conflict in American history.

Peace talks meant to end the fighting began in Paris in May 1968, but the talks broke down and the fighting continued. In 1969, President Richard Nixon began reducing the number of U.S. soldiers in Vietnam. The Green Berets were pulled out of the Central Highlands in the early 1970s and ordered back to the United States. When the last of the U.S. Special Forces were withdrawn from Vietnam in 1971, they had earned 11,790 medals, including 17 Medals of Honor.

Congress eventually cut off funds for the war, leading President Nixon to settle with the North Vietnamese. The war ended in 1975, after North Vietnamese troops had conquered South Vietnam.

Movie hero John Wayne, by starring in the Hollywood film *The Green Berets*, helped build the Green Beret legend.
(Movie Star News)

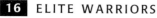

The Green Berets and their achievements were not forgotten. Indeed, they became legendary. John Wayne, one of Hollywood's most popular actors of the day, produced and starred in The *Green Berets*, a film that described the work of the Special Forces in the Central Highlands of Vietnam. There was a bestselling book by Robin Moore also titled *The Green Berets*, as well as "Songs of the Green Berets," by Barry Sandler. There were also countless magazine articles and newspaper features. Of course, many of the films and articles romanticized the subject, giving a less-than-realistic picture of the Green Berets.

Today, the U.S. Special Operations Command includes not only the Green Berets, but also the Naval Special Warfare Command (the SEALs) and the Air Force Special Operations Command. But it is the Green Berets who have gained the greatest renown. The same is true of the green beret itself. Army Airborne troops now wear a maroon beret, while the dress uniform for the Army's Rangers includes a black beret. But it is the green beret that remains the most recognizable and respected headwear in the U.S. armed forces.

A pair of U.S. Navy SEALS, experts in counter-guerrilla warfare, are pictured during Operation Crimson Tide in Vietnam's Vinh Binh province in 1967.
(U.S. Navy)

U.S. NAVY SEALS

The U.S. Navy SEALs are perhaps the toughest and fittest of America's secret warriors. In his book *The Commandos: The Inside Story of America's Secret Soldiers,* Douglas C. Waller calls them "the most physically fit and ferocious warriors in America's military—and perhaps any military in the world."

They have to be tough and fit to do what they do. SEAL teams specialize in commando assaults, underwater demolition, and intelligence-gathering missions. While they excel in any mission that has to do with water, SEALs, more and more, are being used for a wide range of other specialties, including parachuting and helicopter assaults. One of their most noted operations is called the Rubber Duck Op. A SEAL team and its rubber raiding raft are parachuted into the water from a C-130 transport jet. The team members fire up the boat's specially silenced 35-horsepower outboard motor and ride hard for the land, their guns trained on the shore.

The SEALs' most unusual method of transportation is the SEAL Delivery Vehicle (SDV). Launched from either a surface ship or a submarine, the whale-shaped, battery-powered SDV travels beneath the water's surface, carrying four divers a much greater distance at a much faster speed than they would ever be able to achieve on their own. The vehicle is used for reconnaissance missions and underwater mapping and exploration.

All SEALs are experts in underwater diving, of course. They sometimes use an open-circuit system, breathing from a tank of oxygen they carry and exhaling into the water. This is scuba (self-contained breathing apparatus) diving, which is well known. But with scuba there's a potential problem. The bubbles created by the diver's exhalations can be spotted at the surface. So SEALs also become skilled in the use of LAR (Lambertson Amphibious Respiratory unit), a self-contained, closed-circuit breathing system that is strapped across the diver's chest. The diver breathes 100 percent oxygen and his exhaled breath is recirculated within the diving apparatus. There are no telltale bubbles.

The 5,500 SEALs and their support personnel are based in Coronado, California. Like the Army's Special Forces, they operate in small groups of specialists. The standard platoon has 14 to 20 men who can break down into two squads, or boat teams.

The SEALs originated in World War II and trace their roots to the Underwater Demolition Teams (UDTs) that were formed to clear safe lanes for landing craft through German and Japanese beach defenses. The teams were also active during the Korean War, from 1950–1953, helping to prepare for assault landings by clearing harbors and channels.

After John F. Kennedy became president in 1961, he urged all of the armed services to increase their capabilities in the field of unconventional warfare. The Navy, in seeking to carry out the president's wish, turned to the UDTs, virtually its only specialists in guerrilla warfare. The new units were called

SEALs, an acronym for *SE*a- *A*ir-*L*and. The first SEAL team was officially commissioned on January 1, 1962.

From 1966 to 1971, SEAL teams saw extensive combat duty in Vietnam. And, more recently, they were in action during the invasions of Grenada and Panama and in the Persian Gulf War.

No military training course is as difficult and demanding as that offered by the SEALs. The applicants, physically fit Navy men in their late teens or early twenties, must first take part in Basic Underwater Demolition/SEAL (BUD/S), a toughening-up process that stresses running, swimming, and calisthenics. The course lasts six weeks. The final week is called "Hell Week." During the seven days of Hell Week, each student is driven to the absolute limit of his endurance. (No women are accepted for SEAL training.)

"Even if a guy is an absolute physical stud, it doesn't mean that he's going to get through Hell Week," says one instructor. "The sixth week of BUD/S is designed to break everyone down physically. There's little time for sleep but many hours for inflatable boat drills, landings on rocky beaches, low crawls through barbed wire, and runs over and around obstacles. And often during these drills there are bullet and grenade simulators going off around them."

The idea of Hell Week is to teach each candidate to turn off pain and focus on the mission. It is based on the concept that pain can be overcome by sheer willpower, that a student can make his body endure more pain than he ever thought possible.

While individual achievement is stressed during training, teamwork is the chief lesson taught. Students learn that seemingly impossible goals can be reached through the combined effort of a thoroughly trained, highly dedicated, confident group.

The BUD/S training center is a collection of concrete buildings between Highway 75 and the Pacific Ocean in Coronado, California. Over the entrance to the main building, the Phil H. Bucklew Center for Naval Special Warfare, there's an inscription that reads: "The more you sweat in peace, the less you bleed in war." It's a slogan that seems to guide the thinking of all BUD/S instructors.

A central courtyard features the "Grinder," a broad expanse of blacktop where students perform daily calisthenics. At the corner of the Grinder stands a brass bell. At one time, a student wanting to quit BUD/S could do so by ringing the bell. On the ground next to the bell rests a line of white helmets bearing the names of students who decided they could take no more.

Navy officials now believe that forcing a student to walk up to and ring the bell is too humiliating, and the bell is no longer used. There are other ways to file a DOR, or "drop-out request." But the helmets of recent dropouts are still lined up next to the bell.

Another change in recent years makes it wrong for an instructor to punch or otherwise manhandle a student. And any student who is injured during training is given time to heal and then permitted to repeat the course with another class. It used to be that injured students were dropped from the program.

Overlooking the BUD/S training complex is the dive tower, a 50-foot, water-filled cylinder. This is the diving tank where students are schooled in underwater diving using various types of breathing apparatus.

During the first week of training, each day begins at 5:30 in the morning and lasts until late in the afternoon. The hours are filled with trips through the obstacle course, long swims in the ocean, and four-mile runs. One drill is known officially as "surf immersion." Students run in and out of the 60-degree ocean water. Run too slowly and the instructor is likely to make you stay in the water longer. Students call the drill "surf torture."

Six-man teams of students are each assigned a black rubber raft, called an IBS, for "Inflatable Boat, Small." Each boat weighs about 150 pounds. Team members learn to hoist the raft atop their heads and carry it almost everywhere. Some students develop bald spots on the top of their heads from the scraping of the raft. Of course, they also learn how to paddle the raft in the surf.

About half of the students drop out during the first six weeks of training. And half of those who remain fail to make it through Hell Week.

Hell Week begins on Monday morning. As far as the instructors are concerned, Monday morning begins at one minute past midnight. That's when the students are awakened by the voices of instructors screaming commands, the sound of smoke grenades and other explosives going off, and the *rat-tat-tat* of automatic weapons being fired. "Welcome to Hell Week," says a soothing voice over the public address system.

In the hours that follow, there are few breaks for students. After eight hours of intensive drills, the half a dozen or so instructors are exhausted. They're replaced by a second instruction team. After another eight hours, a third team of instructors takes over. But there are no replacements for the students.

At the beginning of Hell Week, students are taught whistle drills. If an instructor blows his whistle once, any student within hearing range must dive to the ground, cover the back of his head with his hands, keep his mouth open, and cross his legs. This is the position that combat soldiers are taught to take when they come under enemy artillery fire. Two blows of the whistle and each student must begin crawling toward the whistle-blower. Three toots and each student must stand. It's up-down-crawl, up-down-crawl, up-down-crawl. Instructors drive students crazy with their whistle drills.

Students spend countless training hours in the mud pit, a 100-foot-long rectangle that is 25 feet deep and is filled at regular intervals with seawater from a hose. The water is allowed to settle, forming a thick layer of mud at the bottom. A barbed wire fence encircles the pit. Students have to slither beneath the wire to get into the pit.

Bizarre drills are staged in the mud pit. Students take part in wheelbarrow races. Each team consists of two men—one walks on his hands, his nose barely above the mud, while his

Members of a
Navy SEAL team
descend from a
helicopter by
rappelling.
(U.S. Navy)

partner grasps his ankles. There are also caterpillar races. In a caterpillar race, the six members of a boat crew sit on each other's laps. Interlocking their arms, the six men seek to move backward as a unit through the muck.

Whistle drills are also held in the mud pit. Two toots on the whistle and each student must hold his breath and bury his face in the mud.

Students are sometimes served lunch during the mud-pit drills, eating while standing hip deep in water and muck. During the meal, instructors set off explosions to simulate grenades and shells. The explosions are real enough to shower the students with dirt and debris.

When the exhausted men who survive Hell Week stagger through the final drills and are informed that they've made it, some laugh or cheer while others weep. They all realize they've endured what few others could possibly endure.

The BUD/S course is merely the beginning. When it's over, each student enters the second phase of training, a seven-week course that teaches the basics of combat diving. This is followed by nine weeks of schooling in underwater demolition, reconnaissance, and land warfare. An additional five weeks are spent at San Clemente Island, where students use the many skills they've developed in real-life situations. Even after graduation, the training continues, for each student receives three weeks of parachute training at Fort Benning, Georgia.

By this time, each man is authorized to wear the Trident, the Navy's Special Warfare insignia. The Trident features an anchor and an eagle with its wings outstretched. In one of its talons, the eagle holds a cocked pistol; in the other, a trident, the three-pronged spear carried by Neptune, the ancient Roman god of the sea.

SEAL teams played an important role in the Persian Gulf War. Iraq's invasion of Kuwait, a tiny oil-rich nation at the northern end of the Persian Gulf, on August 2, 1990, triggered the war. After overrunning Kuwait, Iraq's troops clustered along Kuwait's border with Saudi Arabia. World leaders feared that Iraq would invade Saudi Arabia next.

In an effort to pressure Iraq to leave Kuwait, Allied planes tried bombing Iraqi military and industrial targets. But the Iraqis made it clear they intended to stay in Kuwait.

The Allies then decided to launch a massive ground attack against Iraqi forces. By mid-February 1991, the Allies had assembled some 700,000 troops—including 475,000 from the United States—3,500 tanks, and 2,000 aircraft in the Persian Gulf region. Most of the Allied ground forces were based in Saudi Arabia, awaiting the call to plunge north into Iraq and Kuwait.

The invasion force also included 17,000 U.S. Marines aboard a fleet of amphibious landing ships in the Persian Gulf. In the weeks before the invasion date was set, spy planes and satellites photographed the Kuwaiti coastline in search of a landing site for the Marines.

But the spy planes and satellites were able to provide only a part of the picture. The Marines needed SEAL teams to swim close to the shore to gather intelligence on the number of enemy troops that would be encountered and the types of defenses that had been built. The invasion force also needed information on the slope of the beaches and the firmness of the sand.

Some 260 SEALs, commanded by Captain Ray Smith, were assigned to the Persian Gulf War. From a small base at Ras-al-Mishab, a coastal town in Saudi Arabia about 30 miles south of the border with Kuwait, Smith sent SEAL teams north to inspect the beaches.

Four special warfare Fountain-33 speedboats were used for the missions, each powered by twin 1,000-horsepower MerCruiser engines. These enabled the boats to travel at speeds of up to 40 knots (between 42 and 43 miles per hour). When the water was calm, the speedboats behaved properly and the trip north was relatively painless. But when the seas turned choppy, it was a different matter. The boats would bounce from wave to wave, sometimes soaring several feet into the air. Broken bones could easily result. And when the boats reached their destination along the Kuwaiti coast, some SEALs had to lean over the side and throw up.

SEAL teams hurried north 10 times to scout the Kuwaiti beaches for the Marines. Each mission was filled with danger. The Persian Gulf was bristling with mines, floating explosive charges that could blow a speedboat to smithereens. The speedboats had no mine detection equipment, and there was little sense in posting a crew member as a lookout. With a boat traveling at 40 knots, there would be no time to warn of the presence of a mine. Crew members understood that if a boat struck a mine, they would become the war's first casualties.

Cyclone-class coastal patrol craft are used for shallow-water missions by Navy SEALs.
(U.S. Special Operations Command)

In addition to the mines, the SEALs had to worry about friendly fire. Allied warships were everywhere in the Gulf and they fired upon any Iraqi boat they happened to spot. Before a SEAL mission, Captain Smith contacted all Allied vessels with guns and warned them not to fire on his speedboats. Even so, a Kuwaiti patrol boat did open fire on a SEAL boat with a 50-caliber machine gun. Fortunately, the SEAL boat was not hit.

At one beach scouted by the SEALs, they were spotted by enemy patrol boats and so quickly moved on. At another beach, the SEALs were fired upon by Iraqi soldiers. Still other beaches were so heavily defended that the SEALs didn't even bother to stop.

But on other missions, the SEAL speedboats paused several miles offshore to launch the black rubber rafts each carried. Crew members boarded the rafts and motored to within roughly 200 yards of the coastline. From that vantage point, they would scan the beaches with their night-vision scopes.

Other times, SEALs would leave the rafts and swim toward the shore. Once on the beach or very close to it, the SEALs would lay perfectly still and watch. They noted where the antiship missile launchers were located and counted tanks, trucks, and other vehicles. They also made estimates of enemy troop concentrations. Back aboard their rafts, the men pulled out pocket tape recorders and described everything they had seen on shore.

The SEALs found most Kuwaiti beaches to be heavily mined and defended. This information confirmed what Central Command had suspected, that because of the concentrations of Iraqi men and equipment an amphibious landing would not be worth all the casualties the Marines would suffer. It was decided that the Marines would be used elsewhere.

But Central Command wanted the Iraqis to continue believing that an amphibious assault was coming, that several thousand Marines would soon be storming the shores of Kuwait. A team of SEALs was assigned to plant this idea in the minds of the Iraqis.

Just after dark on February 23, 1991, the day before the Allies were to launch their ground war against Iraq, a pair of SEAL speedboats roared out of Ras-al-Mishab and zoomed north toward Mina Saud, just beyond the Kuwaiti border. When the two boats reached a point about seven miles off the beaches of Mina Saud, the crews killed the engines and then untied three black rubber rafts.

Five men climbed into each raft and traveled to within 500 yards of the shoreline. Two SEALs from each raft then slipped into the water. Each swimmer carried a floatable backpack that was loaded with 20 pounds of explosives. Timing devices on the backpacks were to be set to explode the backpacks at 1:00 A.M. This would give the Iraqi defense forces three hours to react before the ground invasion got under way.

Besides the six swimmers, the three rubber rafts carried a support crew of radio operators, machine gunners, and engine repairmen. Three of the six swimmers were equipped with Heckler & Koch MP-5 machine guns to use if they encountered Iraqi soldiers patrolling the beach. The other three swimmers carried M-16 rifles fitted with grenade launchers to be used against enemy machine gunners. Each of the six also had a pistol lashed to his belt and a knife strapped to his leg.

Pushing the backpacks in front of them, the six swimmers headed for the shore, kicking their fins. Their hands and faces had been blackened with camouflage paint. Beyond the shoreline, the night sky was brightened by exploding bombs from Allied planes and oil well fires set by the Iraqis.

Once the swimmers reached water shallow enough to enable them to stand, they spread out until they were 50 or 60 yards apart. On the beach, there was no sign of life. Each man set the timing device on his backpack so it would explode at exactly 1:00 A.M. The swimmers left the backpacks in about a foot of water, knowing that the tide and surf would carry them onto the beach. Then the men swam back to their rafts.

About a half hour after midnight, the SEALs launched their production. The curtain-raiser was meant merely to awaken the Iraqi defenders. Two speedboats moved in close

Two SEALS prepare to board a SEAL Delivery Vehicle launched from a specially equipped submarine.
(U.S. Special Operations Command)

and started spraying the beach with fire from their .50-caliber machine guns and pounding it with 40-mm grenades. Boat crews also dumped two-pound explosive charges over the sides, which were set to go off every two minutes.

At 1:00 A.M., right on schedule, the knapsacks on the beach started exploding. Each created a deafening roar. Combined with the machine gun fire, the exploding grenades, and the thump-thump-thump of the underwater charges, it sounded like World War II had erupted. The Iraqi defense force had no choice but to believe that the beach at Mina Saud was about to be attacked by thousands of U.S. Marines.

The next day, with the real Allied ground attack successfully launched, the commanding officer of the SEAL commandos who had staged the phony attack received a cable from his commanding officer. "Please pass on to your men an 'extremely well done' on last night's mission," the message began. Not only had the guns and rocket launchers of the Iraqi defenders remained pointed toward the sea, but "elements of two Iraqi divisions" were fooled by the SEALs' charade and reacted to the east toward Mina Saud.

"Pass it on to your men," the message concluded. "Job well done. Bravo Zulu!" which is a Navy expression meaning congratulations.

The charred helmet of a Delta Force commando and the wreckage of a burned-out helicopter lie in the desert sand at the spot where the attempt to rescue American hostages came to a tragic end. *(Wide World)*

3

DELTA FORCE

Kurt Muse, an American arrested in Panama by Panamanian dictator General Manuel Noriega for running an underground radio station, was lying on his bunk in his jail cell at 12:45 A.M. on December 20, 1989, when a burst of machine-gun fire woke him up. Muse looked up fearfully. He had been told by Panamanian soldiers that if any Americans tried to rescue him he would be executed.

Within minutes, Muse heard an American voice. "Moose, you OK?" the voice asked. "Lie down on the floor. We're blowing down the door."

Muse did as he was told to do. An explosion ripped through the cell as the door flew open. An American commando was standing in the doorway. "Follow me!" the man said. "We're going to the roof!"

The two men raced to the roof where a small helicopter was waiting to take off. As the helicopter lifted into the air, it was jolted by rifle fire from Panamanian soldiers. The engine sputtered and the aircraft plunged to the street below, then hopped along the street and into a courtyard.

Panamanian soldiers began peppering the helicopter with more rifle fire. But the commandos, some of them now wounded, formed a ring around the disabled aircraft and fought off the Panamanians until an armored personnel carrier arrived to rescue Muse and the helicopter crew members.

"There were no Rambos," Muse said later. "These guys are just very, very calm, very quiet and very professional."

The rescue of Kurt Muse was part of Operation Just Cause, the American military effort to overthrow the government of Manuel Noriega, head of Panama's National Defense Force. The "very professional" soldiers who performed the rescue were members of Delta Force, the U.S. Army's elite commando unit. With its headquarters at Fort Bragg, North Carolina, Delta Force is made up of about 800 people, most with highly developed, highly specialized skills. They can be ready to depart within an hour on a counterterrorist mission or a commando-style assault anywhere in the world.

The Army is very secretive about Delta Force, refusing to say that the unit even exists. Nevertheless, its name and its mission are well known to the general public, for Delta Force has been popularized in several books and a number of feature films. Chuck Norris is the Hollywood version of what a Delta Force commando looks like.

Delta Force dates back to the early 1970s, when International terrorism was on the rise. American soldiers stationed in what was then known as West Germany found themselves the target of antiwar students turned terrorists. A U.S. Army officers' club in Frankfurt, West Germany, and the headquarters building of the U.S. Army in Heidelberg were bombed.

Hijackings, assassinations, and kidnappings were becoming common. A British airliner was hijacked by terrorists and taken to a desert airfield not far from Amman, Jordan. After the passengers were taken off, the terrorists blew up the airliner, an event that was played out before a worldwide television audience.

The terrorist act that had the greatest impact occurred at the Olympic Games in Munich, West Germany, in 1972. Eleven Israeli athletes were slain by Arab terrorists who rampaged inside the Olympic Village. The murders horrified the world.

Not long after the tragedy at Munich, U.S. military planners came to realize that the United States needed a small, highly trained unit of experienced troops to serve as a counterterrorist force. A gruff Army colonel named Charles "Chargin' Charlie" Beckwith was given the assignment of putting the unit together. Fort Bragg was chosen as its headquarters.

An early volunteer for the Army's Special Forces, or Green Berets, Beckwith had seen service in Vietnam. He was nearly killed there during a rescue operation, taking a bullet in the stomach. After the Vietnam War, Beckwith was assigned to the Special Warfare School at Fort Bragg.

On June 2, 1977, Beckwith was handed the authority to form the 1st Special Forces Operations Detachment, otherwise known as Delta Force. It was to be a small, highly trained counterterrorist unit, meant to deal with kidnappings and aircraft hijackings. Later, its responsibilities would be broadened.

The original concept had also called for an organization of about 1,200 men commanded by a colonel and divided into 16-man units that could be further broken down into four four-man patrols or eight two-man patrols. But there was to be an emphasis on flexibility, so that commandos and units could change roles when necessary.

The first 30 recruits were personally selected by Beckwith. Subsequent recruits were volunteers from other Special Forces units or the Rangers.

Each member of Delta Force was required to be in top-flight physical condition and boast a wide range of skills, everything from parachuting to the repair of wheeled and tracked vehicles, from climbing the sides of tall buildings to hot-wiring cars.

The first volunteers were put through a rigorous series of physical tests to determine that they were qualified. Each man was expected to do 37 sit-ups in one minute and 33 push-ups in one minute, run two miles in not more than 16½ minutes, and, while fully clothed and wearing jump boots, complete a 100-meter (109-yard) lake swim.

Each recruit was also expected to complete a speed march that covered 18 miles through thickly wooded countryside while carrying a 55-pound pack. Any recruit who required more than three hours to complete the march wasn't thought of very highly.

Trainees took part in other "land-navigation exercises," as Beckwith termed them, that were even more demanding. One, conducted in the mountains, ended with a 50-mile march across rugged terrain that had to be completed in 20 hours, with the recruit carrying equipment that weighed 70 pounds. Said Beckwith: "The endurance march revealed clearly those candidates who had character—real determination, self-discipline, and self-sacrifice—and those who did not."

After about 12 hours on such a march, a man would be on the brink of total exhaustion. "What the hell am I doing here?" he would be asking himself. To Beckwith, this was a critical moment. "He [the recruit] would begin to look for excuses to quit, to slow down, even to hope he would injure himself," Beckwith said. "Anything to allow him to stop." For many men, this was the breaking point: they rested too long or slowed their pace to such an extent, it was no longer possible for them to meet the deadline.

"A few others," said Beckwith, "had the sense of purpose, the courage, the will, the guts to reach down inside themselves for that intangible that enabled them to carry on." Those were the men that Beckwith chose for the Delta Force. He called the 50-mile march a "crude" method of evaluation but noted that it was one that the British SAS (Special Air Service) had been using for about 25 years. (Beckwith had spent a year serving with the SAS in the early 1960s.)

By the middle of 1978, 185 volunteers had been tested by Beckwith and his staff, and 53 had been chosen as Delta Force troopers. By the end of the year, 79 additional volunteers had yielded another 20 members.

A key element of most counterterrorist operations is getting the commandos to the scene of the action as quickly and efficiently as possible. There are three possible avenues of approach—by land, air, or sea. For each, specialized equipment has been developed. A good deal of trooper training focuses on this equipment.

For entry by air—that is, for parachuting in—two methods are used: HAHO (high-altitude, high-opening) or HALO (high-altitude, low-opening). With HAHO, a parachutist can open his chute at an altitude of 35,000 feet. It's then possible to "parafly" for distances of up to 30 or 40 miles, yet land with such accuracy that the roof of a particular building can be picked as one's target. HAHO enables the aircraft delivering the chutists to remain outside of radar range or stay beyond the border of a hostile nation. When using HALO, a commando waits until he is approximately 500 feet above the ground before opening his chute.

To bring in the equipment they need, Delta paratroopers rely on CADS (the Controlled Aerial Delivery System). This involves a parachute with a guidance system that boasts a miniature computer. The computer receives signals from a homing beacon that automatically guides the chute to its landing point. The chute can handle loads of up to 500 pounds.

Although attacks from the sea are the specialty of the Navy's SEALs, all Delta Force commandos are trained in scuba and other methods of breathing underwater. Two nuclear submarines, the *Sam Houston* and the *John Marshall,* have been converted for use by Delta troopers. Each submarine can carry as many as 50 fully equipped commandos.

Delta troopers also have to be familiar with many types of airplanes and helicopters. Delta and other special forces are transported by the MC-130H Combat Talon II. The aircraft is equipped with terrain-following radar, an in-flight refueling capability, and communications jammers and other electronic countermeasures that enable the aircraft to fly into and out of enemy territory without being detected.

The MC-130H can also be equipped with STAR (the Surface-to-Air Recovery System). STAR allows an aircraft to pluck a trooper from the ground as it flies by at treetop level. The system works like this: The trooper releases a helium-filled balloon trailing a stout wire that is attached to a shoulder and hip harness he is wearing. As the aircraft glides low over the trooper, a V-shaped frame mounted at its nose engages the wire, which is fed into hoisting equipment at the rear of the aircraft. Slowly, the commando is raised toward the plane's open belly.

Much of each commando's training program involves weapons and shooting. Delta troopers seek to become the best marksmen in the world. But accuracy is only part of the story. A commando has to be able to burst into a room and shoot the

The nuclear submarine *John Marshall* is one of two subs that have been converted for use by Delta Force commandos.
(U.S. Navy)

terrorists there before they can shoot the hostages. He has to move fast. He may only have a part of a second to aim and fire.

Commandos learn "instinctive firing." There is no time for careful aiming. The shooter looks over the top of his pistol, rifle, or machine gun and picks up his target above the weapon's front site, then fires away.

Delta commandos rely on a variety of 9-mm pistols in most hostage situations. But anytime a good number of terrorists are involved and the target area is a sizable one, they turn to a machine gun, specifically the Heckler & Koch MP-5, a German-made weapon that fires 9-mm rounds.

One other weapon must be mentioned. In most assaults involving hostages in an aircraft, a key moment comes when the commando team has to gain entry to the aircraft. What the team has to do is blow in the plane's doors and windows, then rush in to overpower the terrorists before they can kill any of the hostages or blow up the aircraft.

To aid in such situations, Great Britain's SAS developed the stun grenade. Everyone calls it a "flashbang." Packaged in a container the size of a soft-drink can, the flashbang consists of thousands of particles of magnesium combined with explosive compounds of mercury. At the top of the container, a metal ring is mounted. When the commando pulls the ring to detonate the grenade, he also squeezes a safety spoon that temporarily prevents it from exploding. He then tosses it into the aircraft and prepares for the blast.

When the flashbang goes off, the mercury explodes with an ear-shattering roar and the magnesium burns with a dazzling white light. Anyone near the explosion is deafened and blinded for several seconds—long enough for the commandos to move in.

Delta Force troopers practice the use of such weapons and all the other skills required in various kinds of counterterrorism operations at a multimillion dollar training complex at Fort Bragg. It features a three-story "shooting house," nicknamed "the house of horrors," with panels that can be shifted around to change the layout of the living room, dining room, bedrooms, or office. Each room is fitted with pop-up cutouts or moving robots that represent terrorists and hostages. Slide projectors can flash images of bad guys or good guys on the walls, which are fitted with bullet traps that catch and mark each round that a commando fires. A computer keeps track of each man's hits and misses.

One room of the shooting house is the aircraft room. Here, a section of a cabin of a commercial airliner is suspended from the ceiling by steel cables. The seats are filled with dummies posing as passengers.

The training complex and its various stagelike sets enable Delta Force commandos to practice different methods of entry and seizure common to counterterrorist operations. They learn how to kick down a door and use flashbangs to daze terrorists. The learn how to descend by rope—rappel—into second- and third-story windows to attack terrorists and rescue hostages.

The commandos are assigned different roles in these assaults. One man may be in charge of explosives, and assigned to blow open a door or take down an entire wall. A marksman may be given a sniper's role. There are also "door kickers" and "room clearers."

What's vital is that the men work together as a team. There is no room for individual heroics. "We don't want any Rambos," says one instructor, referring to the soldier of almost unbelievable courage and skill created by Hollywood's Sylvester Stallone. Each member of a four-man team must know exactly what he and the other men are going to be doing, where they are going to be positioned, and in what direction each is going to be firing. In this regard, each operation is as carefully planned and rehearsed as an elaborate stage production.

For each operation, commandos are clad in carefully chosen clothing and equipment. Each man wears a gray or black Kevlar helmet over a hood made of flame-resistant Nomex. The helmet can be fitted with a microphone and earphone so a commando can keep in touch with other mem-

For Delta Force warriors, camouflage is often a personal matter.
(U.S. Special Operations Command)

bers of the team. Depending on the operation, each man may also be wearing shatterproof goggles or a chemical mask.

The commando's upper body is shielded by a Kevlar vest, which protects against gunshots and blast fragments. The vest is worn over a lightweight Nomex jumpsuit. He also wears leather gloves and Gore-Tex assault boots.

Each commando's outfit may also include a tactical assault vest. The vest's pockets and pouches hold extra ammunition, a medical kit, a flashlight, a radio receiver, and whatever other items the operation requires.

Some commandos wear additional protection during training sessions in the shooting house. They can, for instance, add knee pads and elbow pads. Also available are various types of body armor to protect the throat and chest, and there are "armored shorts" to protect the groin.

The Delta Force training compound also includes a series of ranges. There's a sniper range where riflemen, or "long guns," as they are called, fire at targets, some of which are more than a quarter of a mile away. At the range for "short guns," commandos fire at targets that are only 50 yards away or closer. There are special pistol, submachine gun, and shotgun ranges. There's a range that's been made to resemble a jungle path along which commandos prowl, keeping alert to fire at pop-up targets. There's a moving-target range where troopers are taught to shoot from speeding cars, or to fire at them as they whiz by. There's also a demolition range for testing various types of explosives.

Recreation hasn't been forgotten. The Delta Force training compound also boasts an Olympic-size swimming pool, a fully equipped gymnasium and weight room, and a basketball court and several racquetball courts.

Early in 1980, Delta Force commandos got the opportunity to test their finely honed skills in a real-world situation. The mission was anything but a success, although the disaster it turned out to be was not the fault of the troopers or their training.

The operation had its origins in 1979, when militant Iranian supporters of the Ayatollah Khomeini stormed the U.S. Embassy in Teheran and took 66 staff workers hostage, including 53 Americans. After diplomatic efforts to get back the hostages failed, President Jimmy Carter ordered Delta Force to come up with a way to rescue them.

What evolved was a complicated two-stage plan. In stage one, four huge AC-130 Hercules cargo planes carrying a 90-man assault force were to take off from an airfield in Egypt and head for "Desert One," an airstrip near Garmsar in Iran, about 250 miles southeast of Teheran. There the big cargo planes were to rendezvous with eight RB-53D Sea Stallion helicopters from the aircraft carrier *Nimitz,* which was operating in the Arabian Sea.

In stage two, the helicopters were to carry the commandos to a hideaway just outside Teheran. As darkness fell, the commandos would board buses and trucks (to be provided by the Central Intelligence Agency, or CIA) for the trip to Teheran. The vehicles were to slip into the city one by one, letting off their passengers at a warehouse that had been secretly acquired by the CIA.

At the appointed moment, the Delta Force commandos were to scale the walls of the embassy, killing or taking captive anyone who attempted to stop them, and release the hostages. Meanwhile, the eight helicopters would have flown to Teheran and landed on a soccer field near the embassy to await the commandos and the freed hostages.

Once the passengers had boarded the helicopters, they were to take off and rejoin the AC-130s at another airstrip, "Desert Two." From Desert Two, everyone would be flown to safety.

The mission turned into an embarrassing failure when two of the helicopters developed engine problems on the flight to Desert One. One of the helicopters had to be left in the desert; the other returned to the *Nimitz.* A third damaged helicopter made it to Desert One but couldn't be repaired and had to be abandoned. With three helicopters out of service, planners felt they had no choice but to scrub the mission.

The mission was not merely a failure. In its final stages, it turned tragic. As the commandos were boarding the AC-130s for the flight back to Egypt, the rotor blade of one of the helicopters knifed into the fuselage of one of the transports. Instantly, flames erupted on both aircraft. Ammunition

began to explode, striking other aircraft. Five helicopter crew members died, and three Americans were killed on the transport. The rest of the crew members and commandos climbed into the remaining transports and the planes took off.

Looking back, critics say the mission was doomed from the beginning because it was so complex. Twenty-one different agencies or units were involved. One of the first rules of such operations is set forth by the acronym KISS, for "Keep It Simple, Stupid."

Beckwith was deeply grieved by what happened. "It was the biggest failure of my life," he said in 1981. "I cried for the eight men we lost. I'll carry that load on my shoulders for the rest of my life." Beckwith died in 1994.

The scorched wreckage of an American AC-130 Hercules at "Desert One" is a sad reminder of the failed attempt to rescue American hostages at the U.S. Embassy in Teheran.
(Wide World)

The catastrophe had enormous impact. In the presidential election that fall, Jimmy Carter lost to Ronald Reagan. Most political observers agreed that the failure of the hostage rescue mission contributed to Carter's defeat. It made American military leaders look inept. They couldn't even keep their aircraft in operating condition or prevent them from crashing into one another. Virtually everyone associated with the fiasco was stung by criticism.

In the years that followed, there were more frustrations for Delta Force. On December 4, 1984, Delta commandos were sent to rescue passengers aboard a Kuwaiti airliner that had been hijacked on its way to Pakistan. Two American passengers were killed and the pilots were forced to fly to Iran. There, both the terrorists and the hostages were released before the commandos had a chance to act.

Just six months later, in June 1985, Delta Force commandos were back in the region following the hijacking of TWA flight 847. After terrorists forced the airliner to land in Algiers, Algerian authorities refused to allow the commandos to launch an assault on the aircraft.

In Panama in late 1989, Delta Force received mixed grades. Before the invasion, Delta commandos were given two missions. One was to rescue Kurt Muse, the American businessman who had been arrested and jailed for running a radio station whose broadcasts were critical of General Manuel Noriega, the head of the Panama Defense Force. The other Delta Force assignment was to capture Noriega.

Delta Force made painstaking preparations. At a remote corner of Elgin Air Force Base near Fort Walton Beach, Florida, those planning the missions directed construction crews in building exact replicas of every home or hideout that might possibly be used by Noriega on the night of the invasion (December 20, 1989). The builders worked from blueprints and drawings of the structures furnished by the CIA. Noriega was also known to use a mountain retreat along the Costa Rican border as a headquarters. At an Army base in Louisiana, a full-scale replica of the mountain home was built. Delta

commandos used these structures in rehearsing their seizure of Noriega.

Those commandos assigned to rescue Muse practiced their mission on a full-scale reproduction of the three-story Carcel Modelo prison in Panama City, where Muse was being held. As the fully armed Delta commandos piled into the building during rehearsals, they were opposed by other commandos who played the part of Panamanian prison guards.

The freeing of Muse went off about as smoothly as could be expected, although four commandos were hurt, one seriously. Muse was rescued without injury.

The attempt to capture Noriega was a different matter. On the night of the invasion, Delta Force commandos stormed all of Noriega's homes and hideaways but came up empty handed. Intelligence agents who had been assigned to keep an eye on Noriega had lost track of him. He had fled to Torrijos/Tocumen Airport, where he spent the night. When he learned that Army Rangers were parachuting into the airport, Noriega got away in a waiting van.

In the days that followed, Delta commandos searched frantically for the Panamanian leader, raiding not only his known hangouts but the homes of his friends and associates. Noriega eventually sought to evade capture by surrendering to the Vatican's embassy in Panama.

After Noriega was finally taken into custody by U.S. authorities, a new civilian government was formed in Panama. But hardly had the problems in Panama been solved when U.S. Special Forces were called into action again. This time the trouble spot was in the Middle East.

During the summer of 1990, Iraq invaded Kuwait. Once having gained control of Kuwait, Iraq threatened Saudi Arabia. An international crisis loomed.

For several months, the United States and its Allies sought to persuade Iraqi president Saddam Hussein to pull his troops out of Kuwait, but he would not. Finally, on January 17, 1991, the Allies launched an air war against Iraq. Its goal was, first of all, to destroy Iraq's ability to launch additional attacks, particularly against Saudi Arabia. With the bombing, Allied military strategists also hoped to wipe out Iraq's ability to produce biological, chemical, and nuclear weapons.

Allied aircraft first bombed Baghdad, the capital of Iraq, and then focused on a wide variety of other targets throughout Iraq and Kuwait. The star of the air campaign was the F-117 stealth fighter, which dropped 2,000-pound laser-guided bombs with pinpoint accuracy. Evening news telecasts featured videos of American bombs plunging down the airshafts and smokestacks of Iraqi buildings. Huge B-52 bombers used unguided bombs in attacking ammunition depots, factories, and warehouses. U.S. Navy attack aircraft flew combat missions from six aircraft carriers in the Persian Gulf and the Red Sea.

Iraq's response to the Allies' heavy pounding was a terror weapon, the "Scud" missile. The Scud was a crude and inaccurate weapon. But when launched by the score toward population centers in Israel and Saudi Arabia, Scuds had the potential to kill and injure huge numbers of civilians and cause widespread fear and panic.

The Scud missiles were also meant to draw Israel into the war. If Israel were to strike back at Iraq because of the Scud attacks, Iraq might then be able to force Arab countries to break away from the alliance by portraying the war as one between Arabs and Jews. But thanks to the urging of the United States, Israel did not enter the war, and the alliance held together.

Allied military planners were aware that Scuds targeted on Israel were located at airfields in western Iraq, and that the missiles aimed at Saudi Arabia were to be found in eastern Iraq. And in the early hours of the war, American F-15Es had destroyed most if not all of these sites and their supply depots. But on the second day of the war, Scuds launched from western Iraq shattered hundreds of apartments in the Israeli cities of Haifa and Tel Aviv. Forty-seven people were injured. In the days that followed, millions of terrorized Israelis, fearing the

Scuds to come might be armed with chemical weapons, remained in sealed rooms with their gas masks close at hand.

It soon became obvious that Allied military planners had seriously underestimated the number of Iraqi Scud missile launchers. And a surprising number of them were mobile launchers, which were kept on the move without letup. A rocket crew would drive, stop, fire and then move on, and do it all within half an hour or so. On February 25, a Scud missile would slam into an Army barracks in Dhahran, Saudi Arabia, killing 28 Americans.

Because Allied bombers were largely unable to destroy the mobile Scud launchers from the air, the attacks continued. General H. Norman Schwarzkopf, who commanded the Allied forces, seemed unable to do anything about the attacks. Bombing the launch sites wasn't doing much good. The only solution seemed to be to destroy the missiles before they were fired.

Back in Washington, General Colin Powell, the chairman of the Joint Chiefs of Staff and Schwarzkopf's boss, felt he had a way to stop the Scuds—a secret force of about 400 men. They included two squadrons of Delta Force commandos, a Ranger company, and a SEAL Team-6 unit. By January 31, the force was setting up its headquarters at Ar Ar, a tiny village in northwest Saudi Arabia, not far from the border with Iraq.

British SAS commandos who already had been active inside Iraq, cutting communications lines and setting up ambushes, helped the Delta troopers get going. The two organizations had worked together closely in the past. It was agreed that the Delta commandos would patrol within Iraq close to the Syrian border, while the British would be responsible for an area to the south, near the border with Saudi Arabia.

By the first week in February, Delta commandos had set up a Scud-hunting routine. Under the cover of darkness, Air Force MH-53J Pave Low or Army MH-47 Chinook helicopters would deliver teams of commandos and their specially equipped land rovers to predetermined sites. Each team would patrol the desert at night in search of Scuds. They would go into hiding during the day. Some Delta teams were able to

Special
Operations
commandos hold
a desert planning
session.
(U.S. Special
Operations Command)

remain on patrol for two or three weeks at a time. Others, after only a day or two in the field, would be discovered by Iraqi soldiers and would have to radio for evacuation by helicopter.

Whenever a commando team discovered a Scud launcher, it would radio an Air Force AWACS (Airborne Warning and Control System) plane, which would then dispatch F-15E or A-10 attack aircraft to demolish the site. The commando team would help direct the attacking aircraft to the target. On their very first night patrol, Delta teams ordered strikes on four Scuds.

In addition to the role they played in the destruction of missile sites, Delta commandos led an assault on a telephone switching station near the Jordanian border that severed landline communications between Baghdad and Amman, Jordan's capital. Delta's helicopters also attacked Iraqi radar sites, command posts, and truck convoys. And on the last day of the war, the Delta troopers helped to destroy 26 Scuds that the Iraqis were planning to launch in a final, last-ditch effort to pull the Israelis into the war.

Trained to infiltrate and fight under virtually any set of circumstances, members of Delta Force typify America's elite soldiers of the 1990s. They are ready to react swiftly and decisively wherever a crisis occurs. Delta Force is regarded by many as one of the nation's best hopes for preserving peace and stability in an unsettled world.

U.S. soldiers stationed in Germany undergo fitness training supervised by Ranger specialists.
(U.S. Army)

4

U.S. ARMY RANGERS

The 75th Ranger Regiment, with its headquarters at Fort Benning, Georgia, ranks as the nation's leading quick-strike force. It can attack by land, sea, or air, day or night. With its great mobility, the regiment gives the United States the ability to put a highly skilled, highly trained military force anywhere in the world within 24 hours.

The primary Ranger mission is to conduct raids or ambushes designed to capture or destroy enemy personnel or equipment. But Ranger battalions can also carry out light infantry missions, which can include capturing airfields or destroying communications centers.

The 75th Ranger Regiment is made up of three battalions: the 1st Battalion at Hunter Army Airfield in Georgia; the 2nd Battalion at Fort Lewis, Washington; and the 3rd Battalion at Fort Benning. About 2,000 men make up the Ranger force.

Ranger officers and enlisted men are drawn from the Army's airborne units, that is, they've been trained as parachutists. It's said that one must volunteer four times in order to become a member of the 75th—first, you must join the Army itself, then sign up for airborne training, then join the Ranger Regiment, and then agree to go to Ranger School.

All Ranger volunteers are put through a vigorous three-and-one-half-week training program designed to screen out those who can't measure up. Recruits must complete an eight-kilometer (4.9-mile) run in 40 minutes. There are road marches ranging in distance from six kilometers (3.7 miles) to 12 kilometers (7.4 miles), which must be completed at ever increasing rates of speed. For all marches, recruits must carry a full pack and all weapons.

About 40 percent of all volunteers wash out. But those who fail yet continue to show enthusiasm for the Rangers and maintain a positive attitude are permitted to try a second time.

After the three-and-a-half weeks of schooling, the new Rangers are assigned to their battalions for operational training, which is tough and stressful and often conducted under simulated battlefield conditions using "live" ammunition.

Rangers train 48 weeks a year, much more than any other Army unit. Training exercises stress physical endurance and extended exposure to the elements, to the wind, rain, and cold. Troops go for long periods without sleep. But the training also puts an emphasis on leadership and teamwork.

Every Ranger battalion follows a cycle in which jungle, mountain, and desert training are conducted at least once a year. And each battalion trains at least twice every three years in extreme cold. All the training is meant to produce the best light infantry force in the armed forces of the United States, perhaps in the world.

The Rangers have a long and rich history. In fact, the use of military units specially trained in scouting and frontier defense predates the American Revolution. In 1756, 20 years before the American colonies declared themselves to be free and independent of English rule, Lord Loudoun, who commanded British military forces in America, wrote to his superiors in London: "It is impossible for an Army to act in this country without Rangers; and there ought to be a considerable body of them."

At the time, the English government and its colonies were engaged in the final struggle with the French for control of the North American continent. Called the French and Indian War, it had begun in 1754 and lasted until 1763.

Modern Ranger history begins with World War II. General George C. Marshall, the Army's chief of staff, decided the United States needed a commando-type organization, a small fighting force specially trained for making quick, destructive raids against enemy-held strongholds. But U.S. military units didn't want to use the word "commando" in naming the force because it was already being used by the British, so they called the force "Rangers." Known officially as the 1st Ranger Battalion, the unit began training at Carrickfergus in Northern Ireland in June 1942. Several other Ranger battalions were formed as the war progressed.

To be selected for Ranger training, a soldier had to show determination, good judgment, and leadership qualities. He needed skills in self-defense, weaponry, mountaineering, seamanship, and small-boat handling.

At Carrickfergus, the men were trained in military tactics against units of British commandos who represented enemy soldiers. The British soldiers tossed grenades and fired small arms over the heads of the Ranger trainees to give them a taste of battlefield conditions.

Throughout the training period, the Rangers used a "buddy system," that is, they worked in pairs. Partners lived together, had their meals together, and endured the bullet and bayonet training together.

By the fall of 1942, the first Rangers were ready for action. They took part in Operation Torch, the invasion of French North Africa, in November of that year. Once Allied forces had gained control of North Africa, they moved quickly to take advantage of their victory, landing in Sicily in July 1943. They then used Sicily as a springboard for invading Italy. Rangers played a role in both the Sicilian and Italian invasions.

By November 1943, Allied forces in Italy had reached a line about 75 miles south of Rome. But there the Germans held fast and the Allied advance stalled. The Allies then tried to maneuver around the Germans by landing troops near Anzio, 33 miles south of Rome.

In the early morning hours of January 22, 1944, Ranger units under the command of Colonel William O. Darby went ashore at Anzio. There was little resistance and some Rangers were ordered to move out from the beachhead and seize the town of Cisterna di Lattoria. But the Germans launched a fierce counterattack and Rangers who had started to advance inland got cut off from their command post.

What happened next was brutal. Germans drove their tanks to the edge of a ditch in which Rangers had taken shelter, lowered their guns, and fired. They pulled some men from the ditch and formed them into a ragged line that they used as a shield as they advanced toward American lines. Very few Rangers survived the ordeal.

Allied soldiers, supported by artillery, tanks, planes, and naval gunfire, eventually brought the German counterattack to a halt. In the weeks that followed, Allied forces reorganized. They attacked from the Anzio beachhead in the spring and drove the Germans toward Rome.

On D-Day, June 6, 1944, when the Allies stormed ashore along the Normandy coast of France, Ranger units were assigned to land with the first waves of assault troops at Pointe du Hoc, about four miles west of Omaha Beach. At Pointe du Hoc, 100-foot cliffs rose like a sheer wall from the narrow strip of sand the Rangers were to occupy.

The first men ashore took shelter in the shell holes produced by German artillery. High seas drenched the Rangers and their equipment, including the ropes and rope ladders they planned to use in scaling the cliffs. The ropes were equipped with special grappling hooks that were meant to dig into the ground. Using special launchers aboard their landing craft, the Rangers planned to shoot the ropes to the crest of the cliffs. But the ropes, soaked with water, were too heavy for the

Men and assault vehicles storm the Normandy beach of France on D-Day, June 4, 1944. *(Wide World)*

launchers to propel them any distance. Finally, the Rangers got a hand-held launcher to do the job.

When the first Rangers struggled to the top of the cliffs, the Germans peppered them with hand grenades. The Rangers eventually got enough men on the cliff to organize an attack and move inland. But the Germans counterattacked and pushed the Rangers back to the cliff. The Rangers radioed for naval gunfire to blast the Germans and help them hold their position. Eventually, a second Ranger unit worked its way toward the Rangers at Pointe du Hoc to bring relief to the besieged unit.

Through 1944 and into 1945, other Ranger units were sometimes used as regular infantry in the continuing assault on Hitler's "Fortress Europe." In the Pacific, Rangers also participated in the retaking of the Philippine Islands from the Japanese. But the most noted of all Ranger units in World War II saw action in the China-Burma-India theater of operations. Commanded by Brigadier General Frank D. Merrill, the unit won fame as "Merrill's Marauders."

The unit came into being after President Franklin D. Roosevelt called for volunteers to take part in a "dangerous and hazardous" mission. The men who were to make up Merrill's Marauders were airlifted to India in 1943 for special training in marksmanship, scouting, and jungle navigation. But they were scarcely prepared for the conditions they encountered in northern Burma, where they did most of their fighting. It was a land of towering mountains and deep valleys, most of them covered by thick jungle growth. Bamboo grew so densely that tunnels often had to be hacked through it. Rangers who crossed rivers or streams on foot would emerge with their bodies covered with blood-sucking leeches. During the torrential rains of the monsoon season, roads become impassable and soldiers slipped and stumbled in the mud.

Despite the horrific conditions, Merrill's Marauders became known for their fast movement. On the march, they used some of the tactics common to Rogers' Rangers. For example, a reconnaissance platoon always moved ahead of the main body of troops, sometimes several miles ahead. A rifle company was next in line. The unit's command center and medical detachment was at the center of the group. Toward the rear came another rifle platoon and heavy weapons.

Late in February 1944, the Ranger unit joined forces with Chinese troops to begin a series of operations meant to cut the chief Japanese supply lines. The Rangers advanced through the thick jungle for several weeks, completing a harsh 100-mile march to surprise the Japanese by blocking their only supply line in the Hukawng Valley. By this time, many of Merrill's men were suffering from combat fatigue and tropical diseases.

Although not nearly at full strength, the unit was ordered to take Myitkyina Airfield and the nearby town of the same name on the Irrawaddy River. The original force of some 3,000 Rangers had been reduced by one-third by this time. Most of casualties resulted not from enemy fire but from exhaustion and a lack of medical treatment. Because of a shortage of supplies, the men often went hungry. A veteran of the expedition said, "Two conditions existed: one in which we felt unfed, and the other in which we *were* unfed."

Nevertheless, the Marauders pressed the attack against the enemy, marching through steep, narrow ravines and scaling the Kumon Mountains. With the help of Chinese reinforcements, the Marauders took control of the airfield at Myitkyina in mid-summer of 1944.

After the Myitkyina operation, Merrill's Marauders were disbanded. Merrill himself was in poor health and died in 1945. But the unit managed to establish a reputation for toughness and determination that was later to inspire Ranger operations in Korea and Vietnam and other parts of the world.

In the Korean War, which lasted from 1950 to 1953, North Korea, supported by Communist China, fought South Korea, which was aided by the United States and other United Nations countries. The Rangers infiltrated enemy lines to attack enemy command posts, artillery positions, and communications centers. These were essentially the same tasks that Ranger units were assigned during the Vietnam War, the longest war in

Frank Merrill (right) with Lieutenant General Joseph Stilwell, the commander of the American forces in the China-Burma-India theater during World War II. *(Wide World)*

which the United States has taken part. U.S. military involvement in Vietnam began in 1950 and did not end until 1975.

In Vietnam, a typical Ranger mission lasted from five to seven days and involved a six-man team that would be placed behind enemy lines by helicopter or boat. The men slept little while in the field and carried everything they needed on their backs. Once it had completed its mission, the team would head for a predetermined landing zone for "extraction" by helicopter.

Late in 1983, Ranger units were assigned to play a major role in the invasion of Grenada, an island nation in the West Indies. The United States targeted tiny Grenada for an attack because President Ronald Reagan feared that Cuba had ambitions to turn Grenada into a Communist state, from which it could export Communism to other islands in the West Indies and to Central America. Reagan's concern deepened when Cubans began building on the island a runway that was judged to be big enough to handle long- range bombers and transport planes from the Soviet Union. The U.S. Marine Corps, the Navy's SEALs, the Army's Delta Force, and units of the 82nd Airborne Division also took part in the invasion of Grenada, which was known as Operation Urgent Fury.

Airborne Rangers were given the task of securing the airfield under construction at Salines in southwest Grenada. They also were instructed to protect the lives of nearly 600 students, most of them Americans, at the St. George's School of Medicine, not far from the airstrip.

Almost as the operation began, things started to go wrong. While the Rangers were in the air approaching the island, it was decided they would parachute in rather than land normally. But none of the men were wearing parachutes. This meant that as the plane circled, the Rangers had to re-rig for a drop, ditching nonessential gear and getting into their chutes. The Rangers were supposed to be on the ground before first light, but because so much time was required to get ready, the drop did not take place until after daybreak.

As the first two MC-130H Hercules aircraft approached the runway, they were met by small-arms fire. The two planes, radioing that they were under "heavy fire," roared away from the jump zone after releasing only a dozen Rangers. Those men spent several terrifying moments on the ground by themselves before a third MC-130H dropped a support team and its equipment. It took two hours to land the first Ranger units, an operation that should have been completed in about half an hour.

Once on the ground, the Rangers began to clear the airport runway of the trucks and oil drums that had prevented it from being used. Later in the day, the MC-130Hs returned to land and unload jeeps, motorcycles, small helicopters, and other equipment.

Another Ranger unit, assigned to assault Richmond Hill prison, ran into real trouble. Built on the site of an old fort, the prison overlooks the town of St. George's, Grenada's capital. The plan called for UH-60 Black Hawk helicopters to hover

over the prison while the Rangers, with full packs and using a "fast roping" technique, slid down ropes to reach the ground in less than 10 seconds. But intelligence had failed to report the presence of two antiaircraft guns on the ridge above the prison. When the helicopters came into view, the guns opened fire. One helicopter was shot down. Another crashed after running out of fuel. The assault on the prison had to be abandoned.

At the end of the first day, the Rangers had joined with units of the 82nd Airborne Division at the airfield and the True Blue campus of the medical school. But these successes had been costly. Five Rangers had died; six had been wounded.

While the Rangers and the 82nd Airborne were occupied at the airfield, Marine Corps units had helicptered in to capture Pearls Airport, the island's commercial airport, on Grenada's eastern shore. Another Marine force launched an amphibious landing at Grand Mal Bay, north of the capital of St. George's. The next day, as the Rangers, with the help of helicopter gunships, expanded the area they controlled, the Marines advanced toward St. George's. The small Grenadan Army did almost no fighting. Resistance came from a force of less than a thousand Cubans, most of whom were lightly armed construction workers.

One of the final engagements took place at Calvigny Barracks, where Cuban-trained troops were believed to be housed. Air strikes by AH-1 Cobra gunships and Navy A-7 fighter jets backed by naval gunfire severely damaged the barracks before the Rangers in UH-60 Black Hawks were ordered to move in.

The Black Hawks came in fast, one right behind the other. The first helicopter landed safely. A second also put down without any problem. But in attempting to land, a third helicopter piled into the second one, from which Rangers were disembarking. When the pilot in the fourth helicopter saw the tragedy unfolding below, he veered sharply to the right and ended up in a ditch. In less than a minute, three Rangers were killed and several were severely injured by whirling propeller blades. And, as it turned out, the barracks had been abandoned by the enemy.

After several days, U.S. troops were in complete control of the island. The people of Grenada welcomed the Americans as their saviors. The next year, 1984, a democratically elected government was restored to power.

It's correct to say that Operation Urgent Fury achieved its goal. But on close examination, the operation was not as successful as it seemed to be. The United States put together a massive force that included a carrier battle group, the latest attack aircraft and helicopters, a Marine amphibious unit, elite Rangers and airborne units, plus state-of-the-art satellite communications. The opposition included less than a thousand Cubans, only about 50 of whom had any military training, and some 2,000 Grenadan soldiers, who were reluctant to fight. Yet the United States suffered almost 200 casualties—29 men were killed, 152 were wounded. Seventy-one Cuban and 100 Grenadan troops were killed. Forty-five civilians died and 358 were injured.

What happened in Grenada helped to force the Department of Defense to create the Special Operations Command. Since 1987, the Rangers have been a part of that command. Along with the Green Berets and the SEALs, they now stand as the nation's first line of defense in the often troubled post–Cold War world.

The MH-53J Pave Low, the most advanced helicopter in the world. *(United Technologies Sikorsky Aircraft)*

5

U.S. AIR FORCE SPECIAL FORCES

Officially known as the MH-53J Pave Low, it is the most sophisticated helicopter in the world. It is so technologically advanced, it takes six crewmen to fly it and operate its specialized electronic gear.

During the invasion of Panama in 1989, Pave Low pilots attacked strongholds of the Panamanian Defense Forces and helped rescue American hostages at the Torrijos-Tocumen Airport. In the opening minutes of the Persian Gulf War, two teams of two Pave Lows, using their radar and high-tech sensors, led an assault force of Army AH-64 Apache gunships that destroyed a pair of Iraqi early-warning radar stations. In so doing, they created a wide corridor through which allied bombing planes could pour without being detected. Within minutes after the Pave Lows and Apaches had completed their mission, the bombers were on their way to attack targets in

Baghdad and elsewhere in Iraq. Pave Lows have also conducted secret rescues in Central America and pursued drug traffickers in the Caribbean.

The Pave Lows are only one of six different types of rotary and fixed-winged aircraft operated by the U.S. Air Force's Special Operations Command, which has its headquarters at Hurlburt Field near Fort Walton Beach, Florida. More than 11,000 people make up the command. It is their job, using the more than 100 aircraft they operate, to get the Army's and the Navy's special forces units to where they're going. Often they must take their aircraft deep into enemy territory under the worst flying conditions.

The Pave Low helicopter dates back to 1980, when U.S. Special Forces were seeking to rescue American hostages being held in Iran. Helicopter pilots and their aircraft were assigned a key role—and made a mess of it. Eight helicopters, RB-53Ds from the carrier *Nimitz*, which was operating in the Arabian Sea, were to rendezvous with six huge Hercules transport planes at a secret airstrip in the Iranian desert. The transports were carrying close to 100 commandos. The RB-53Ds were then to helicopter the commandos to a hideaway not far from Teheran, where the hostages were being held. But two of the helicopters broke down on their way to the airstrip, and a third one arrived in a damaged condition. The mission had to be scrapped as a result.

The botched rescue attempt made it clear that the U.S. military required dependable helicopters suitable for long-range operations. To satisfy that need, the Air Force rebuilt its CHH-53 Super Jolly Green Giant and called the new helicopter the MH-53J Pave Low.

The MH-53J Pave Low is a $40 million helicopter with a single rotor and a twin-turbine engine. It can fly hundreds of miles at night in the worst flying weather, evade enemy radar by traveling at low altitude, and elude enemy air defenses with its electronic jammer and flare and chaff dispenser. Armor-plated, the Pave Low can be armed with either three 7.62-mm cannons or three .50-caliber machine guns.

The Pave Low's crew consists of two pilots, two flight engineers, and two aerial gunners. It takes eight months of training to become a pilot. Four months are necessary just to learn to fly the aircraft. One problem is the Pave Low's size. The aircraft is so much bigger than conventional helicopters that student pilots constantly overshoot their landing zones. And in the Pave Low, the pilot's vision is limited. When hovering to land, the pilot has to be "talked down" by other members of the crew. He doesn't know he's landed until he senses that the aircraft's wheels have touched the tarmac.

Pave Low trainees not only learn how to fly the aircraft at night as most helicopter pilots do, using night goggles and standard navigation systems, they also learn how to "pave" at night. This means learning how to use the precision navigation equipment that enables the Pave Low to fly for hundreds of miles at tree-top level in good or bad weather.

Like almost all other aircraft (and most boats and ships), Pave Low helicopters use the Global Positioning System (GPS) as a navigational aid. Using information from 18 satellites orbiting the earth, GPS tells the pilot exactly where he is on earth at any given moment. It also tells him the course to steer to reach his destination.

For the Pave Low pilot, GPS is only the beginning. The helicopter is also equipped with the Enhanced Navigation System, a package of the most sophisticated navigational aids available. The package includes a ring laser gyroscope that operates with laser light beams and mirrors to sense the movement of the helicopter over the earth's surface. It feeds its readings into a computer that then figures out the helicopter's exact position, its speed, and the direction in which it's heading.

Near the pilot's right knee is a circular, green-glowing screen called the "Projected Map Display." On the screen appears a map of the terrain over which the Pave Low is flying. The screen also shows the helicopter's path across the map. It's like something produced by Nintendo.

The Pave Low pilot also keeps checking a pair of round radar scopes. One is for the terrain following/terrain avoiding radar. It produces an electronic pathway on its scope. If the pilot keeps the helicopter within that pathway, he gets electronic climb and dive commands. He knows that if he follows the commands, he can be confident he won't hit anything.

The second radar scope is for the forward-looking infrared radar, or FLIR (called "fleer" by helicopter crew members). It picks up the infrared energy that comes from the ground and translates it into images on the cockpit screen. Even on the darkest nights, the pilot and other crew members get a picture of what's outside.

By the time he's completed training, a Pave Low pilot is able to fly at speeds of up to 150 miles an hour, relying only on his radar scopes and cockpit instruments, and land his aircraft on a designated target the size of a throw rug hundreds of miles away. And he's able to do it at night, in bad weather, and perhaps while eluding enemy surface-to-air missiles.

Other aircraft operated by the Air Force's Special Operations Command include the following.

• *MC-130H Combat Talon II.* A transport plane that flies parachute commandos on long-range secret missions, the

With a range of 3,100 miles and a crew of nine, the MC-130 Combat Talon delivers paratroopers and their equipment at faster speeds and with greater accuracy than was ever before possible.
(U.S. Air Force Special Forces Command)

Combat Talon is equipped with forward-looking, terrain-following (or terrain-avoiding) radars that allow for low-level flight. The aircraft is thus able to avoid detection by enemy radar. Specialized onboard radar and computers make it possible for the aircraft to locate even the smallest drop zone and deliver equipment and supplies with great accuracy, night or day. High-speed deliveries, necessary in hostile territory, are another of the aircraft's specialties.

The Combat Talon is also equipped with STAR (the Surface-to-Air Recovery system), a unique method of retrieving one or two people at a time or containers weighing as much as 500 pounds from land or water. The person to be recovered puts on a protective suit that has a lift line attached to it. At the other end of the line, there's a helium-filled balloon that he releases. The Combat Talon, traveling at about 150 miles an hour, intercepts the lift line, plucking the person from the ground. Winches on the aircraft reel the person aboard. The entire operation takes less than 10 minutes. The person lifted aboard is said to feel less shock than that experienced during a parachute drop.

The Special Operations squadron of Combat Talons is based at Hurlburt Field. The plane is capable of speeds in excess of 300 miles an hour. Its crew includes two pilots, two navigators, two loadmasters, an electronic warfare officer, a flight engineer, and a communications specialist.

• *AC-130 Spectre Gunship.* An airborne artillery unit whose chief role is to deliver concentrated firepower with pinpoint accuracy, the Spectre made a vital contribution during the invasion of Grenada in October 1983. The aircraft was also called upon in December 1989 for Operation Just Cause, the invasion of Panama, again to provide firepower in support of U.S. forces.

The Spectre is armed with two 20-mm Vulcan cannons, each capable of firing 2,500 rounds a minute; a 400-mm Bofors cannon that fires 100 rounds a minute; and a 105-mm howitzer, a short-barreled cannon that can fire up to four rounds a minute.

Capable of speeds of more than 300 miles per hour, the AC-130 holds the record for the longest flight by a C-130 aircraft–29.7 hours. Of course, with in-flight refueling the aircraft has an unlimited range. The Spectre's crew of 13–four officers and nine enlisted men–includes a pilot, a copilot, a navigator, a fire control officer, a flight engineer, a low-light TV operator, an electronic warfare officer, an infrared detection set officer, and five aerial gunners.

- *HC-130 N/P Combat Shadow.* This is an aerial tanker, providing in-flight refueling for helicopters used to transport special operations forces. Its crew consists of a pilot, a copilot, a primary navigator, a secondary navigator, a flight engineer, a communications system operator, and two loadmasters.

- *EC-130E.* Packed with electronic equipment, the EC-130E is used for jamming enemy radars or in psychological warfare operations. For example, during the Persian Gulf War the aircraft was used as a radio station, broadcasting up to 18 hours a day to Iraqi soldiers. The broadcasts often explained the advantage of surrendering and how to do so (by waving a white flag or turning the gun barrel of one's tank to the rear).

Blade antennas are mounted on each side of the plane's fuselage and beneath each wing. Bullet-shaped cannisters are also mounted beneath the wings. These house antennas are extended several hundred feet behind the aircraft during flight.

The aircraft's crew includes two pilots, six electronic equipment operators, an electronic warfare officer, a navigator, a flight engineer, and a loadmaster.

Flying chiefly at night, the HC-130 N/P Combat Shadow provides air refueling for special operations helicopters.
(U.S. Air Force Special Operations Command)

• *MH-60 Pave Hawk.* The newest of the Air Force's helicopters, the Pave Hawk, filled with advanced navigation and communications gear, is designed to deliver special operations personnel on missions inside hostile territory. It is also equipped to resupply such missions.

The Pave Hawk can travel up to 350 miles without refueling, or it can be flown to any part of the globe by C-141 or C-5 airlifters. It operates with a crew of three—two pilots and a flight engineer.

Air Force Special Operations Forces originated in World War II. They've been active in every war since, including Operation Just Cause in Panama in 1989 and 1990, and the Persian Gulf War in 1990 and 1991. During the last 50 years, the command has also played a role in countless human-assistance and nation-building missions in virtually every part of the world.

An SAS trooper keeps watch over Argentine prisoners at Goose Green in the Falkland Islands.
(Wide World)

6

GREAT BRITAIN

Not long before daybreak on the morning of May 15, 1982, Griff Evans, a sheep farmer in a tiny community on Pebble Island, one of the more than 100 Falkland Islands in the South Atlantic off the southern tip of Argentina, was awakened by the sound of loud explosions. Evans peered out of a bedroom window to see the night sky aglow with exploding ammunition and oil drums at a nearby airstrip used by the Argentine Air Force.

As Evans busied himself in the kitchen making coffee for himself and his wife, he was unaware that Pebble Island had been occupied by two 16-man units of Great Britain's Special Air Service (SAS) Regiment and that SAS troopers had fired the opening shots in the British effort to retake the Falklands following an Argentine invasion early in April of that year.

As Evans and his wife watched anxiously, the conflict got hotter. SAS specialists placed explosive charges on the 11

Argentine aircraft parked on the grassy airstrip. Then the destroyer *Glamorgan* got into the act. As the ship's guns began to boom, the shells zeroed in right on their targets, thanks to an artillery observer with the SAS team. The shelling resulted in the destruction of the Argentine aircraft and a radar station, which could have been used to help guide Argentine bombing planes sent to attack the British Task Force.

Members of the SAS force had arrived at Pebble Island by helicopter, shinnying down ropes, an exercise they had practiced for weeks on the flight decks of task force aircraft carriers. After they had completed the destruction of the aircraft and the radar station, the troopers exchanged gunfire with Argentine soldiers assigned to defend the airstrip. Two troopers were wounded in the clash, which ended when helicopters picked up the men and carried them back to their ships.

By June 14, the Falklands had been liberated. The SAS played a major role in the British triumph. SAS commandos provided intelligence and reconnaissance reports for para-troopers and ground forces who landed after them. They infiltrated Argentine strongholds at night to kill sentries.

Some reports say that SAS units were even active in mainland Argentina, where they attacked airfields, although these reports have never been verified. And when, in 1979, the Soviet Union began a long, grim struggle to take over in Afghanistan, the SAS was said to have been involved, surreptitiously observing and evaluating Soviet military tactics.

Special Air Service Regiment

The United Kingdom, which consists of Great Britain and Northern Ireland, is a small country, about the size of the state of Oregon and with a population about one-fifth that of the United States. Its soldiers, sailors, marines, and airmen have taken part in more than 50 military campaigns since the end of World War II. Their major involvement has been in Northern Ireland, where violence and terrorism have continued for about three decades.

Time after time in recent years, Great Britain's armed services have shown the ability to respond quickly and vigorously to acts of international terrorism. In such instances, the Special Air Service has won the highest praise. Indeed, the organization has been hailed as the world's toughest antiterrorist commando unit.

Founded during World War II in the Libyan desert, the SAS had as its early goal operating behind enemy lines in North Africa. The organization did so with great success. The SAS was credited with destroying hundreds of Nazi aircraft on their own airfields, freeing countless Allied prisoners, and blowing up scores of enemy ammunition storage depots.

The SAS was disbanded after World War II but was revived in 1952 to fight Communist rebels in Malaya. In 1958, SAS commandos came to the aid of the sultan of Oman, whose country was threatened by terrorists supported by Saudi Arabia.

The SAS of today is made up of three regiments, each of which averages between 600 and 700 men. Unlike the elite forces of some other nations, the SAS does not seek to recruit directly from the public. Instead, the organization draws applicants from the British Army. Those who apply are put through a hellish trial and training period that lasts for three to four months, with each man's physical and emotional strength tested to the breaking point.

The first weeks of the course stress physical fitness and map reading. Small groups of men are sent into the rugged Brecon Mountains of southern Wales in fog or at night with only a map and a compass with which to navigate. Tremendous stamina is required. One "sickener," as he is called, tells a recruit who has just arrived at his destination after a long and difficult trek that he must immediately return to his starting point. "That finishes a lot of them," says one observer.

Toward the end of the course, recruits must complete a grueling 40-mile hike over rugged mountain terrain. Each man carries a rifle and a 55-pound pack. The hike must be completed in 20 hours. No wonder that 80 to 90 percent of the original applicants fail to complete the course.

In subsequent training for the small handful that have survived, four-man teams practice reconnaissance, sabotage, and ambush techniques. They are also taught how to resist interrogation at the hands of an enemy, with questioners stopping just short of actual physical torture.

In another phase of training, recruits learn to live off the land. This test goes a bit beyond the ability to camp out overnight and snare a rabbit or have the willingness to dine, perhaps, on certain types of mountain greenery. Each recruit is sent into a tough piece of countryside equipped with only a knife and a box of matches. His assignment: survive for five days while seeking to avoid "capture" by SAS instructors who are trying to hunt him down.

The final phase of training, what some recruits look upon as the "fun" part of the course, is parachute training. Each man must make seven jumps, three of them with full equipment and one of them at night.

Even after one wins admission to the "regiment," as it is called, and receives the beige beret with its winged dagger badge, the training continues, with each man learning more-specialized skills. These depend on the type of unit that a man joins. It breaks down like this: the three SAS regiments are divided into four squadrons, known as "Sabre Squadrons." Each Sabre Squadron is divided into four 16-man Troops. There are Boat, Air, Mountain, and Mobility Troops.

Boat Troops learn canoeing and small boat handling, plus underwater diving with either scuba or oxygen-rebreathing gear. They're also schooled in the techniques of beach reconnaissance and underwater demolition.

The men who choose the Air Troop learn advanced parachuting techniques. Being dropped during the day or at night from a C-130 Hercules at 30,000 feet and several miles from their ultimate objective is considered a "normal" operation. But Air Troops are also trained in high-altitude, low-opening (HALO) and high-altitude, high-opening (HAHO) jumping.

Mountain Troops get special training in skiing, rock and ice climbing, and high-altitude survival. They learn how to utilize "snowholes," burrowing deep into the snow to create spaces where they can shelter themselves from the wind and conceal themselves from the enemy. The air they breathe comes from holes they poke in the room's "ceiling" with their ski poles.

Mobility Troops become experts in vehicles. They learn to drive, maintain, and repair not only many types of cars and trucks, but also a wide range of armored personnel carriers and infantry fighting vehicles. And their expertise extends not merely to vehicles used by the British Army but to those of other countries as well.

Some troopers spend a period with the Army, learning how to fly helicopters. Troopers with a special gift for languages may attend the Army's language school. Some of these men later join the Army's Intelligence Corps, or "I" Corps, sometimes called the "eye-spy" corps.

SAS Commandos practice assault boat landings in 1982 in preparation for fighting in the Falkland Islands.
(Wide World)

Although the military leaders of many nations have looked upon the SAS as one of the toughest and most professional of all elite forces, the organization was little known to the general public for many years. That situation changed in May 1980, when SAS troopers were called upon to respond to an act of terrorism that was watched by millions on television as it was actually taking place.

Six masked gunmen who claimed to be Iranian Arabs had seized the Iranian Embassy in London and were holding hostage 24 men and women, mostly Iranians. The terrorists threatened to blow up the five-story building and kill the Iranian hostages unless the Iranian government agreed to their demands. These included the release of 91 political prisoners being held in Iran by the followers of the fanatical Ayatollah Khomeini.

Government leaders in Iran seemed willing to allow the hostages to be killed rather than accept the demands of the terrorists. "We are ready to accept the martyrdom of our children in England," the Iranian president declared. "We will not give in to blackmail."

London police decided to handle the standoff with patience. Their goal was to wear down the terrorists until they realized they had no hope of winning and surrendered.

But waiting was no easy job. Noisy crowds gathered at the scene, including Iranian students who were led by a fanatic with a bullhorn. They chanted, "Long live Khomeini" and "Death to Carter" (Jimmy Carter, the president of the United States at the time). Another group beat drums and danced for peace. A cluster of Britons sang "Rule Brittania." A London newspaper said the streets were being turned into "a battlefield for other people's quarrels."

Meanwhile, inside the embassy, when one of the prisoners managed to get to a telephone, the terrorists shot him. Then they dumped the body outside the embassy's front door.

With the killing, British authorities changed strategy and decided to send in the SAS. Troopers had been preparing for the call to action. From the roof of the embassy building, they

A police negotiator, his arms held wide, walks away from the Iranian Embassy in London after delivering a note to gunmen holding hostages. *(Wide World)*

had lowered microphones on cables down the chimneys in order to pinpoint exactly where the hostages were being held and where each of the terrorists was stationed. Earlier, they had arranged for a work crew with heavy pneumatic drills to begin tearing up a nearby street. The racket was meant to mask the sounds the troopers were making on the roof.

Careful planning preceded the actual assault. Three teams of four men each would do the job. One team would go in from the balcony of the building next door to the embassy. A second team would descend from the roof on ropes and burst through windows at the rear. A third team would smash through a wall the embassy shared with the building next door. The bricks had been carefully removed from the wall, leaving in place only a thin sheet of plaster.

The three SAS teams were armed with tear gas, frame charges to shatter the windows, and stun grenades (which the Army calls "flashbangs"). The troopers' chief weapon was the Heckler & Koch MP-5 submachine gun, a 9-mm weapon with a pistol grip and a telescoping metal stock whose compactness makes it ideal for use in confined spaces. The "Hockler," as it is nicknamed, can fire up to 800 rounds per minute.

Early on a warm May evening, the troopers launched their attack, figuring that the terrorists would not be expecting to be hit while it was still daylight. At a signal, all three teams swung into action. There was one hitch. One member of the team descending from the roof got his rope snagged. This prevented the other team members from using their frame charges, since they didn't want to injure their colleague. So they simply kicked in the windows and tossed flashbangs into the room. Flashbangs cause total confusion and are not meant to do any harm.

As troopers burst into the embassy's rear windows, a terrorist raised an automatic pistol and took aim. But one of the hostages flung himself at the terrorist, distracting him. A trooper then shot the terrorist.

On the second floor, a group of 15 hostages were terror-stricken by the explosions and gunfire. Two terrorists

Bullet holes in the plate glass front doors of the Iranian Embassy in London following a six-day siege and the hostage rescue led by the SAS.
(Wide World)

ran into the room and began shooting into the group. One Iranian official was killed and two others were wounded. But when the terrorists realized how hopeless their situation had become, they threw down their weapons and sought to mingle with the hostages, hoping they wouldn't be discovered. Their strategy failed. The troopers recognized the terrorists and shot to kill. Only one of the terrorists managed to surrender.

The entire operation took about 11 minutes. It ended with the hostages being led to safety from the embassy, where several small fires had been started. From beginning to end, all had unfolded before British television cameras as millions watched in awe.

Performing on television was a great rarity for members of the SAS. The organization prefers to remain shadowy and mysterious, keeping its operations cloaked in the greatest secrecy. Even when the heroes of the Iranian Embassy rescue raid were decorated for their bravery and skill, the ceremony was held in the tiny hamlet on England's border with Wales where the SAS has its supersecret headquarters, and the names of those honored were never made known to the British people or the world at large.

Overseas, as noted earlier, SAS troopers were involved in the campaign to suppress Communist rebels in Malaya in the early 1950s. They also joined in the fighting that took place from 1963 to 1965 to help prevent the uniting of Brunei and Sarawak into a new Communist state. From Southeast Asia, they shifted their attention to the Middle East, first to Aden (now North and South Yemen) and then to Oman. Since 1976, they have been involved in the strife in Northern Ireland, where terrorist groups seek a united Irish Republic. And SAS troopers fought in the Falkland Islands. During the Persian Gulf War, SAS commandos crossed from Saudi Arabia into Iraq and started operations a full week before the air war began (on January 17, 1991). Patrolling in their stripped-down Land Rovers, they cut Iraqi communications lines and set road ambushes. When Iraqi artillery units began firing Scud missiles into heavily populated areas of Israel, SAS troopers were assigned to seek out and destroy the missile launching sites.

Through the years, the SAS has won a reputation for being one of the smartest and toughest elite forces any nation has produced. The organization shows no reluctance in sharing its knowledge and techniques with friendly nations. So it is that America's Green Berets, Germany's GSG9, and the Special Forces of Australia, Belgium, and New Zealand are all, in some measure, in debt to Great Britain's SAS.

Special Boat Squadron

During World War II, the British created dozens of military units to perform specialized tasks. The SAS was one such organization, and one of only two to retain its identity to the present day. The other is the SBS, the Special Boat Squadron, a 650-man unit.

The chief role of the Special Boat Squadron is to inspect possible landing sites for major amphibious operations, a task assigned to the unit during the war in the Falklands Islands in 1982. A team of SBS commandos, flown to the South Atlantic in a C-130 Hercules, parachuted from the aircraft to a waiting submarine, and from the sub made its way to shore in inflatable boats.

SBS recruits are selected from the Royal Marines and then undergo rigorous training. Although recruits spend many weeks becoming skilled in underwater swimming, navigation, and canoeing, and other such arts, they also learn the same HALO and HAHO parachuting techniques as their counterparts in the SAS and U.S. Special Forces. They are taught how to exit from a submerged submarine. They also practice infiltrating from helicopters, fixed-wing aircraft, and merchant and naval ships.

The Commachio Group

Formed in May 1980 with the primary task of guarding Great Britain's offshore oil rigs in the North Sea, the Commachio Group, like the Special Boat Squadron, is composed of Royal Marines. In recent years, the group's responsibilities have been expanded to include counterterrorist attacks and ship assaults. The Commachio Group is based in Scotland and numbers about 400 officers and men.

Lufthansa

Jürgen Schumann, the pilot of the hijacked Lufthansa airliner, is menaced with a pistol as the aircraft sits on the airfield at Aden before the flight to Dubai and then Somalia. Schumann was later killed by the hijackers.
(Wide World)

7

GERMANY

On October 13, 1977, four Palestinian terrorists—two Arabic-speaking men and two women—armed with hand grenades, automatic pistols, and an assortment of explosives hurried past the light security at Palma Airport on the Spanish island of Majorca to board Lufthansa Flight 181, a Boeing 737 bound for Frankfurt, West Germany. Most of the passengers aboard the plane were vacationers who were homeward bound after having spent carefree days lounging in the western Mediterranean sun.

Minutes after the plane took off, the terrorists pulled out their pistols and grenades and ordered the pilot to change course. During the next five days, the aircraft flew to Rome, where it was refueled, then to Cyprus in the eastern Mediterranean, then to Bahrain in the Persian Gulf, then to Dubai on the southern shore of the Persian Gulf, and on to Aden, a port city on the Gulf of Aden.

The terrorists, who identified themselves as representing the BaaderMeinhofgang, demanded the release of 11 leaders of that organization who were being held in jails in West Germany. (West Germany merged with East Germany in 1990 to form a united Germany.) They also wanted $15 million in cash. In exchange, the terrorists promised to give up the passengers and crew members they were holding hostage. They said they also would release Hanns-Martin Schleyer, a West German industrialist who had been kidnapped six weeks earlier.

But if their demands were not met, the terrorists were ready to act ruthlessly. In a message to West German chancellor Helmut Schmidt, they said, "Any attempt on your part to delay or deceive us will mean immediate execution of Hanns-Martin Schleyer and all the passengers and crew of the plane."

While in Aden, the terrorists carried out a savage act of violence. Jürgen Schumann, Flight 181's captain, convinced the terrorists that he should leave the plane to inspect the nose wheel, which he believed might have been damaged during the landing. Once outside the aircraft, Schumann made a bold dash for the control tower to give the police descriptions of the terrorists and their weapons. The hijackers were furious. They said they would blow up the aircraft if Schumann did not return at once. The captain felt that he had no choice but to go back, and he did.

An enraged Walter Mahmud, the terrorist leader, was waiting for Schumann at the plane's door. He pointed his pistol at Schumann and screamed, "Are you guilty or not?" He forced the pilot to kneel in the aisle between the passenger seats. Then he put his pistol to Schumann's face and killed him with one bullet.

The next morning Mahmud forced the copilot, Jurgen Victor, to fly on to Mogadishu, the capital of Somalia, on the east coast of Africa. After the plane had landed, the terrorists dumped Schumann's body out onto the taxiway.

Until the murder of Jürgen Schumann, the West German government was prepared to negotiate a peaceful end to the hijacking. But the pilot's death, the government was told, was likely to be only the first. Once the killing had begun, it was a good bet that it would continue.

But the West German government was prepared with an alternative plan. It had established GSG9 as a special unit to combat terrorists. When the highjacking of Flight 181 took place, GSG9 was called into action.

As the hijacked aircraft made its way across the Mediterranean Sea and Saudi Arabia to Mogadishu, it was trailed by a plane carrying 30 GSG9 commandos. A second plane with 31 additional troopers and the unit's commander, Ulrich Wegener, later joined the chase.

Great Britain's Special Air Service (SAS) had provided the West German commandos with ultrasensitive listening devices that could be used to locate the terrorists within the hijacked plane. The British had also furnished a supply of stun grenades, or "flashbangs," which exploded in a burst of sound and light to immobilize the enemy for several seconds. Two SAS experts went along to supply on-the-scene assistance.

In Mogadishu, the behavior of the hijackers became more and more menacing. At one point, they tied the passengers' hands behind their backs with stockings. Then they doused the passengers with liquor from the airplane's supply lockers. They apparently thought that the alcohol in the liquor would help to fuel the flames once they set the plane afire.

The terrorists later untied the hostages after they had received a radio message from West German negotiators saying that the government was willing to meet one of their demands and release the 11 prisoners and fly them to Mogadishu. "It's seven hours flying time from Germany," Walter Mahmud told the passengers he was holding captive. "I will give them seven hours."

Meanwhile, the first of the two aircraft carrying the GSG9 commandos had landed at the Mogadishu airport under the cover of darkness. The rescue operation was under way.

Less than an hour before the terrorists' final deadline, Somali soldiers, under instruction from the commandos, built a bonfire on the runway several hundred feet from the hijacked plane. The fire was meant to distract the terrorists and draw them into the plane's cockpit, away from the hostages seated in the passenger section. The plan seemed to work, for two terrorists were spotted looking out of the cockpit window.

With the terrorists distracted, 28 commandos, their faces blackened and their bodies camouflaged, crept up to the

Hostages freed by GSG9 commandos leave the plane that brought them back to Germany from Mogadishu.
(Wide World)

hijacked plane. Silently, they placed rubber-coated aluminum ladders at the plane's sides so they could approach the emergency exits over the wings. Seconds later, they blew open the exits and tossed their flashbangs into the cabin. *"Hinlegen! Hinlegen!"* ("Lie down! Lie down!") the troopers shouted as they poured into the aircraft.

Within seconds, the hostages began streaming through the emergency exits. One of the female terrorists opened fire from the passenger compartment and was shot and killed instantly. The other woman was shot in the thigh and later taken to a hospital in Mogadishu. Mahmud and the other male terrorist threw grenades before they, too, were shot and killed. Fortunately, the grenades exploded under cockpit seats and did not injure any of the troopers or passengers.

Eight minutes after the operation began, Ulrich Wegener, who directed his commandos from beneath the aircraft, was able to announce "Springtime" over the radio, the code word that the aircraft was in the hands of the GSG9. One commando, one flight attendant, and four passengers were slightly injured. Except for the murdered Captain Schumann, all of the crew members and hostages survived.

GSG9

Until its highly successful mission at Mogadishu, GSG9 was not well known, not even in West Germany. GSG9, or Grenzschutzgruppe Neun (Border Protection Group Nine), to use its full name, was formed in 1972 following the massacre of nine Israeli hostages by their five Palestinian captors at the Olympic Games in Munich. The man chosen to bring the unit into existence, and who was to serve as its first commanding officer, was Ulrich Wegener, a quiet but tough long-time officer of the German border police. Wegener's military experience dated back to the closing days of World War II, when, at the age of 15, he was pressed into service with the Luftwaffe, the German Air Force.

Ulrich Wegener,
the commander
of GSG9, responds
to reporters'
questions after ar-
riving in Cologne,
Germany,
following the
hostage rescue.
(Wide World)

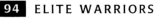

Wegener chose his commandos from the 20,000-member border guards, the military unit he knew the best. The first 60 volunteers were put through two days of physical and psychological testing, followed by a rigorous 13-week training course. Only about 20 percent managed to pass.

Those that remained became skilled in swimming, diving, and mountain climbing, and received 140 hours of training in karate. The trainees also spent up to four hours a day practicing with a variety of weapons, including sniper rifles, Heckler & Koch MP-5s, and other automatic weapons.

At GSG9 headquarters in St. Augustin near the city of Bonn, volunteers studied the tactics of terrorist organizations and the use of sophisticated listening devices, including directional microphones. They learned how to pick locks or blow them apart, and how to impersonate flight attendants and mechanics. Many recruits went on to take the German Army's basic and advanced parachute course.

Today, GSG9 maintains a force of between 160 and 200 men, organized in six units of 30 men each. Each unit includes demolition and ammunitions experts, and advisors in psychological warfare as well. The 61 troopers under Wegener's command at the Mogadishu airport included 28 men from one action group, a back-up unit, and a handful of other support personnel.

At the time the hostages were freed, German radio and television stations interrupted their regular programming to announce the news. Later, when the hostages and the commandos returned to Germany, they received a heroes' welcome and were honored with speeches and parades.

But the celebrating was cut short when police announced they had found the body of Hanns-Martin Schleyer in the trunk of an abandoned car in the French town of Mulhouse. In a warning to the German government, Schleyer's killers sent a message to a Paris newspaper that declared, "The battle has just begun."

Schleyer's death brought to ten the number of victims murdered by terrorists in West Germany during 1977. The number included Jürgen Schumann, the captain of the hijacked jet.

GSG9's operations are limited to counterterrorism. Members of the unit are trained to take part in assaults on aircraft and embassies, provide protection for VIPs, and carry out undercover work against terrorist groups.

Each GSG9 volunteer gets a thorough psychological examination and is put through a series of other tests to determine his intelligence and physical ability. Senior officials with the unit say that it takes from two to three years for a recruit to become fully trained. There is no maximum enlistment period for members of GSG9. As long as an individual remains fit, he can continue as a member. Although the average age of members is 29, few remain with the unit after reaching the age of 40.

GSG9 members wear the standard forest green uniform of Germany's border guards, but it bears the white GSG9 badge that depicts the German eagle surrounded by oak leaves.

Each member is issued two sets of weapons, one for day use, the other for night fighting. Included are a 9-mm pistol, a .357-caliber pistol, a Heckler & Koch MP-5 machine gun, and a Heckler & Koch 7.62-mm sniper's rifle with both laser and thermal-imaging sights. Each man also gets a pump-action shotgun with solid-shot ammunition to be used in breaking down doors.

For road transportation, GSG9 commandos rely on Volkswagen minibuses or Mercedes sedans. Neither of these are fitted with armor, because armoring would mean added weight, and GSG9 prefers speed to protection.

When GSG9 was proposed in the early 1970s, many people in West Germany, including government officials, shunned the idea of creating an undercover security force. It brought back memories of the SS, the Nazi Party's elite military unit, and the Gestapo, Germany's secret police during the Nazi regime. But Ulrich Wegener was able to overcome the opposition. The German government provided him with a sizable budget to form his elite corps and saw to it that he was supplied with the most modern antiterrorist equipment available. What's happened since then seems to indicate that the decision was justified.

Following a combat operation in Crete in 1941, a German mountain trooper receives a decoration.
(Bundesarchiv/ Koblenz)

1st Gebirgsjager Division

In their World War II planning, Germany's military leaders realized that the war in Europe would involve mountain warfare that required a special type of fighting man. Mountain

warfare might be the toughest fighting in the world. To capture a nearby mountain peak can require an exhausting trek into a valley followed by the tortuous ascent to the summit, often under fire and the harshest weather conditions. Tough and hardy, often from the Alpine regions of the country, German mountain troops fought in virtually every major campaign of the war–in Poland, Scandinavia, France, the Balkans, Russia, and Africa.

Mountain troops were equipped with special short skis that were essential for fast movement. Snow goggles were another necessity. For crossing glaciers, the men wore crampons, metal plates fitted with iron spikes that attached to the bottoms of their shoes.

Food had to be high in calories but low in bulk. It had to be capable of being cooked quickly or eaten raw, because cooking at high altitudes requires more time and more fuel than at lower altitudes. Dried meats, dried fruits, and dehydrated vegetables were standard fare. Chocolate and grape sugar were everyday snacks. Drinking water was obtained by melting ice or snow.

Mountain troops learned to construct their shelters out of whatever material happened to be available. This usually meant they dug caves out of snow or ice. In mountainous areas, where high winds made cave building virtually impossible, soldiers would try to make a single wall of stone and then take shelter behind the wall. The more fortunate ones sometimes were able to use a Finnish plywood shelter, which could be taken apart and transported by pack animal from one site to the next.

In these primitive shelters, candles carried by each soldier provided light. At company headquarters, kerosene lamps were preferred to electric light because it was much easier to obtain kerosene, a by-product of petroleum, than light bulbs.

Mountain troops often used one type or another of local animal as a beast of burden, to pull a small cart laden with supplies and equipment. In the Caucasus, the towering mountain range in the former Soviet Union between the

Black Sea and the Caspian Sea, mountain troops relied on small mountain donkeys. Each could carry a load of up to 85 pounds. The donkeys were also esteemed because they required little food. Also in the Caucasus, the 1st and 4th Mountain Divisions used the two-humped Asian camel as a pack animal. And over the frozen terrain of Lapland, a region that embraces the northernmost stretches of Norway, Sweden, Finland, and the former Soviet Union, the reindeer was widely used by mountain troops.

Communication between units of mountain troops was often a problem. Mountain peaks and unusual atmospheric conditions frequently blocked radio reception. Signal flags became the standard method for transmitting messages from one unit to another. Their greatest drawback, of course, was their limited range. Even on the clearest days, a signaler was visible for no more than five miles.

Avalanches were a more serious problem. Mountain troops had to be skilled in map reading and weather forecasting in order to avoid hazardous terrain or cross it without endangering their lives. Standard procedure was to first lay out a trail, which usually zigzagged down a slope or along a ridge. Traveling straight down a mountain could trigger a disaster.

Once a trail had been decided upon, troops would divide into groups. The first group would cross the hazardous stretch and stop when it reached safe ground. Then the second group would follow, then the third, and so on.

The artillery used by mountain troops had to be capable of being taken apart easily, and the individual parts had to be light enough so they could be carried long distances by soldiers on skis or by pack animals. As for each soldier's weapon, rifles fitted with telescopes were widely used. This was because the increased visibility provided by the clear mountain air allowed the enemy to be seen over much greater distances. In effect, every mountain soldier was a sniper.

Today, the tradition of troops specifically trained in mountaineering, skiing, and endurance marching continues with the 1st Gebirgsjager Division. The division includes the 23rd

Gebirgsjager Brigade, a Special Forces unit trained in guerrilla and antiguerrilla warfare. Like those mountain soldiers of generations past, the men of the 23rd Brigade are skilled and experienced in every aspect of mountain and arctic warfare—in skiing and mountaineering, and in surviving the hazards of blizzards and avalanches.

Approximately 4,000-men strong, the 23rd Brigade has been entrusted with the defense of the Bavarian Alps in southern Germany. In carrying out this responsibility, the brigade would assume a "stay behind" role; that is, following an enemy occupation, members of the 23rd would vanish into the mountains to carry out a prolonged period of guerrilla warfare.

Because of its special role in Germany's defense, the 23rd Brigade is the only unit in the modern German Army that is permitted to drink beer at lunchtime. It could well be the only military unit on the face of the earth to be so honored.

French troopers study maps at Kolwezi's Impala Hotel, which was used as a headquarters by Kantangan rebels during the 1978 uprising in Zaire.
(Wide World)

8

OTHER NATO COUNTRIES

Signed in 1949 by the United States, Canada, and a number of Western European nations, the treaty that led to the creation of the North Atlantic Treaty Organization (NATO) provides that an attack on any one of the members is to be looked upon as an attack on all members.

At the time, much of Western Europe was fearful of being attacked by the Soviet Union. The hope was, of course, that the powerful Soviets would think twice about launching an attack against Western Europe, knowing that they would have to fight the United States, too.

The breakup of the Soviet Union in 1991, and the fact that the Soviets and Soviet-led nations no longer represented a military threat, led to important changes in NATO. A new "strategic concept" was announced. It stated that NATO military forces of the future were to be smaller, have greater mobility, and be capable of being expanded quickly by the calling up of reserve units.

The Special Forces units of several NATO nations pretty much follow those specifications. This chapter describes some of those elite forces.

Belgium

Similar to the U.S. airborne Rangers, Belgium's Para-Commando Regiment (the Régiment Para-Commando) is the nation's principal Special Forces unit. The regiment consists of

Belgian paratroopers in Stanleyville in 1964 display a machine gun captured form Congolese rebels.
(Wide World)

three battalions with supporting artillery, antitank, and armored reconnaissance units.

Since its founding in 1952, the Para-Commando Regiment has been called upon frequently to subdue violence in the African republic of Zaire, which became an independent nation in 1960. Before gaining its independence, Zaire was a colony of Belgium and known as the Belgian Congo.

In 1964, after rebels had slaughtered thousands of Congolese and taken dozens of whites hostage, Belgian commandos parachuted into the Stanleyville (now Kisangani) airport to restore order and permit the evacuation of the Belgian population. In 1978, the Para-Commando Regiment returned to Zaire, this time to aid in the rescue of Europeans in Kolwezi whose lives were threatened by a rebel force that had slipped into the country from neighboring Angola. In that operation, Belgian commandos fought side by side with units of the French Foreign Legion's 2nd Foreign Parachute Regiment.

Belgium also has a specially trained counterterrorist unit, the Escadron Spécial d'Intervention. The unit protects senior government officials and suggests methods for improving the security of embassies in foreign nations.

Canada

Although Canada's Special Service Force is capable of fighting anywhere in the world, its specialty is mountain and arctic warfare. The unit does its training in the rugged, snow-covered mountains of northern Canada.

The Special Service Force was created during World War II. The unit was first formed as a parachute battalion and became part of Great Britain's 6th Airborne Division and the combined U.S.-Canadian Special Service Force. Both of these units were dissolved at the war's end.

The Special Service Force was re-created in 1972, with its headquarters in St. Hubert, Quebec. The unit's muscle comes from the 750-man airborne regiment that often conducts joint exercises above the Arctic Circle with Great Britain's Royal Marines and Norwegian and Dutch forces.

Members of the Special Service Force are equipped with M-16A2 rifles, Belgian 7.62-caliber and American .50-caliber machine guns, plus TOW (tube-launched, optically-tracked, wire-guided) missiles. Accurate, powerful, and long-ranged, TOW missiles are a prime antitank weapon.

In addition to the parachute regiment, Canada's Special Service Force includes armored, artillery, and airmobile infantry regiments. There are also smaller engineer and signal units.

The parachute regiment is on standby alert 365 days a year, meaning it could be in action within 48 hours. The other regiments can be mobilized within another 72 hours.

France

During the 1980s, France reorganized the French Army and created a rapid deployment force known as the Force d'Action Rapide. With some 47,000 men, the Force d'Action Rapide consists of five divisions plus a number of smaller units, including the French Foreign Legion's world-renowned 2nd Foreign Parachute Regiment (2e Régiment Etranger de Parachutistes).

The 2nd Regiment consists of some 1,300 officers and men divided into six companies. Their responsibilities cover everything from urban warfare to mountain and arctic fighting, from demolition and sabotage to sniping and antitank warfare.

During the last two decades, the 2nd Regiment has performed several missions in such troubled African nations as Chad, Rwanda, and Djibouti. Two companies of the 2nd Regiment are posted on a full-time basis on the islands of Réunion and Mayotte in the Indian Ocean. Still another contingent is stationed on the equator in South America, guarding the Kuru Space Center in the Republic of Guyana. The installation has been called "Europe's most precious asset in the space race."

The battle song of the 2nd Regiment begins with the words, "We are the men of the shock attack." Recent history supports that description.

The 2nd Regiment's paratroopers demonstrated their fast-attack capability in 1978, when some 2,000 Katangan rebels attacked the mining town of Kolwezi in the Republic of Zaire, driving Zairean troops out and keeping them out. Once in control, the rebels began looting shops and homes and brutalizing the population. Europeans were hunted down to be terrorized or shot.

France and Belgium agreed to send in troops to quell the violence. Jimmy Carter, America's president at the time, placed the 82nd Airborne Division on alert. Then it was decided that no American troops would be sent to the war zone. Instead, U.S. transport planes would be used to ferry fuel and supplies to Zaire for use by the French and Belgians.

The French called upon the 2nd Foreign Parachute Regiment to intervene. On the morning of May 18, the first units flew out to Zaire from the regiment's headquarters on the island of Corsica. The regiment's vehicles and heavy weapons were airlifted to the trouble zone by American transports.

Dropped over Kolwezi after a four-hour flight, the paratroopers immediately seized key positions and dug in. The first night, the rebels launched a fierce attack but the paratroopers were able to beat it off. Reinforcements arrived the next day. Soon after, the paratroopers launched an attack of their own, killing hundreds of rebels and chasing the survivors back across the border into Angola. Five paratroopers were also killed. By the first week of June, peace had been restored to Kolwezi and the 2nd Regiment was back in Corsica.

The town of Kolwezi was a shambles after the fighting. No one could escape the scenes of destruction and death. An estimated 1,000 Africans died. Almost 100 whites were massacred.

But many hundreds of Europeans had been saved by the French and Belgian paratroopers. Said one survivor, "If the

A French paratrooper guards weapons stacked at an airport in Kinshasa, Zaire.
(Wide World)

paratroopers had not come to our rescue, you would have seen killing on a scale you never dreamed of."

France's Force d'Action Rapide has been hailed as a tough, "go anywhere" unit that always manages to get the job done. The 2nd Foreign Parachute Regiment goes a long way toward helping the force maintain that reputation.

Italy

Italy has probably suffered more from terrorism that any other European nation. As a result, several different counterterrorist units have been organized by the Italian military and police to deal with the problem.

The Sub-Aqua Raider Commando Group (Commando Raggruppamento Subacqui ed Incursori), known by the acronym COMSUBIN, is one of the most important, if not *the* most important. Much the same in character as the U.S. Navy's SEALs and Great Britain's SBS (Special Boat Squadron), COMSUBIN, with about 200 members, not only serves an antiterrorist function but can handle such assignments as beach reconnaissance, mine-clearing, and sabotage of enemy port facilities.

COMSUBIN has a rich history. Italians, after all, were among the first to practice scuba diving and were quick to apply what they had learned to underwater warfare. During World War II, when the Italians fought on the side of Germany and Japan as one of the Axis powers, Italian "frogmen" attacked Allied shipping in the harbors of Alexandria, Egypt, and Gibraltar.

Members of today's COMSUBIN are highly skilled and trained. Training begins with a rigorous 10 months of endurance tests and with some schooling in marksmanship and the use of explosives. This is followed by 42 weeks of Ranger and parachute training before qualifying.

The favorite weapon among COMSUBIN members and those of Italy's other Special Forces units is the Beretta 9-mm M12 submachine gun. Slightly smaller than Israel's Uzi or Germany's Heckler & Koch MP-5, the Beretta features a selector switch that gives it either single-shot, three-round burst, or fully automatic capability. It can be fitted with a 20-, 30-, or 40-round magazine. The weapon has a firing rate of about 500 rounds a minute and an effective range of about 100 yards.

The AR70, of recent design, is a lightweight version of the Beretta M12. Instead of 9-mm ammunition, the AR70 uses 5.56-mm rounds. It takes either 20- or 30-round magazines. An extremely accurate weapon, the AR70 can be converted for use as a sniper rifle with the addition of a telescopic sight.

Formed in 1952 and given its present name in 1978, the Folgore Brigade is Italy's principal airborne assault force. In the event of war, the brigade would be assigned responsibilities similar to those of the U.S. Airborne Rangers, including behind-the-lines raiding and reconnaissance. In addition to their parachuting skills, members of the Folgore Brigade are highly trained and skilled in mountain warfare techniques.

The Netherlands

One of the Special Forces units of the Netherlands is known as the BBE (Bizondere Bystand Eenheid, or "Different Circumstances Unit"). In addition to being responsible for combating terrorism, the unit is trained in riot control, so its members can be called upon to assist the Dutch police in times of crisis.

A Dutch soldier mans a heavy machine gun atop an armored personnel carrier near a train hijacked by South Moluccan terrorists.
(Wide World)

Composed of just 90 men, the BBE got a chance to demonstrate its skills for the Dutch and the rest of the world during several weeks in May and June of 1977, when South Moluccan terrorists hijacked not a plane but a train near the village of De Punt. They also seized control of a school at Bovensmilde. The terrorists were seeking independence from Indonesia for the Pacific island of South Molucca. They also called for freedom for 21 other South Moluccans who had been jailed for previous acts of terrorism.

The hijacking of the train was not the first such act of its type by South Moluccan terrorists. Two years earlier, they had hijacked another train. But that time the terrorists had given up without a struggle after a 13-day siege. This time it was different. The terrorists had shot the train's engineer to show that they meant business.

Despite the shooting, the Dutch government seemed to be in no hurry to settle the skirmish. Dutch psychiatrists manned telephones around the clock, talking to the gunmen about food and supplies they needed for themselves and the hostages, but at the same time trying to negotiate a peaceful settlement with them. Police in armed vehicles ringed both the train and the school.

All the while, the BBE was preparing for action. A small canal, shielded by a dike, passed near the train. At night, BBE Marines, trained in the use of scuba gear, swam to within 15 yards of the railroad cars. They then crept up under the first part of the train, where the terrorists had their headquarters, and planted listening devices. These enabled the BBE to monitor the hijackers' conversations and become acquainted with their day-to-day routines.

The Marines also studied the hijackers' faces from photographs taken with telescopic lenses. And a few miles away, they began practicing their assault on an exact replica of the hijacked train.

It became a war of nerves that lasted for almost three weeks. The hijackers dropped their demand that the 21 other Moluccan terrorists be granted their freedom. They also re-

leased 105 children and one of the teachers they had held at the school, but they kept four teachers as their captives. And they still held 55 passengers aboard the train.

On June 11, the Dutch government decided the time had come to break the stalemate and ordered the BBE Marines to attack. The operation began just as dawn was breaking, when a pair of F-104 Starfighters, flying wingtip-to-wingtip, made a low-level pass over the train. The ear-splitting noise and the vibrations stunned the terrorists and hostages alike. At the same moment, 30 Marines stormed the train. Some placed plastic explosives against three of the train's doors and also blew huge holes in the sides of the cars. Marines rushed aboard screaming at the hostages to keep down.

For almost 20 minutes, the sound of gunfire echoed through the countryside. Cows in green meadows were terror-stricken and stampeded out of fear. When it was over, two hostages and nine terrorists lay dead. Only one Marine was wounded.

The assault on the school was easier. A Dutch armored personnel carrier began the attack by bursting through a brick-and-glass wall of the school. Then the Marines surged in. They obviously had caught the terrorists off guard, because three of them were in their underwear. Within minutes, all four terrorists were in handcuffs and the four teachers were freed unharmed.

Only one part of the daring rescue effort did not go as planned. Teams of doctors and psychiatrists had been assembled to treat the freed hostages, who were expected to be suffering from serious physical and emotional problems after spending almost three weeks in captivity. Arrangements were made for them to spend their first 24 hours of freedom in the hospital. There, it was planned, they could relax, eat good food, and talk over their experiences with professional counselors. But the freed hostages, most of whom were in good shape, had no wish to spend another night away from their families. All they wanted to do was go home.

An Israeli soldier stands beside an Israeli flag atop the ruins of Beaufort Castle in Lebanon in 1982.
(U.S. Navy)

9

ISRAEL

In the early morning hours of June 27, 1976, sleepy passengers boarded Air France Flight 139 at Athens International Airport, where the aircraft had stopped briefly on its way to Paris. Few people noticed the German lawyer and his girlfriend who settled into seats in the first-class section, or the two Arabs who were flying tourist class.

But minutes after the plane took off, the German woman stood in the aisle beside her seat, held two hand grenades above her head, and shouted, "Sit down!" Then she herded the frightened passengers into the tourist section of the airplane, where the pair of Arabs was already in control. At the same time, the woman's companion produced a pistol and took over the flight deck.

The man and the woman were members of the German Baader-Meinhof group, while the two Arabs belonged to the

PLO, the Palestine Liberation Organization. What they wanted was the release of 53 fellow terrorists held in prisons in France, Germany, Israel, Switzerland, and Kenya.

The terrorists forced the crew to fly to Libya, where the plane was refueled (and a pregnant passenger was allowed to go free). Then the plane flew to Entebbe airport in Uganda, an East African nation ruled by the dictator Idi Amin, whose five-year reign of terror was thought to have cost the lives of as many as 200,000 Ugandans. Although Amin presented himself to the world and to the hostages as a mediator who wanted to bring about a peaceful settlement of the situation, he was anything but that. Amin seemed, in fact, to be a partner in the hijacking. Upon landing at Entebbe, one of the hijackers had remarked, "Everything is OK. The army is at the airport." In the terminal, Amin had warmly embraced the hijackers.

The 246 passengers were forced into an old terminal building and placed under guard. During the next few days, many of the passengers were released. But 104 passengers, those with Jewish names or Israeli passports, were held as hostages. They were made to remain in the terminal, sleeping at night on wooden benches or concrete floors as rats scurried about them.

As soon as news of the hijacking reached Israel, the elite units of the Israeli Defense Forces went on full alert. Meanwhile, the hijackers announced that the hostages would be killed and the jet blown up unless the 53 terrorists were released.

The Israelis drew up three plans for liberating the hostages. The first involved dropping commandos and their equipment by parachute on nearby Lake Victoria, and then attacking the airport by amphibious assault. A second plan called for an all-out attack on the airport from Kenya, Uganda's neighbor to the east, with which Israel had good relations. The third option was a bold airport raid, with the commandos arriving by military transport planes.

Those planning the operation chose the third option. It seemed to offer the best chance of reaching the airfield without being detected, rescuing the hostages, and getting home again.

The terminal at Entebbe where the passengers were being held had been built by an Israeli firm, and the construction plans were thus easily available. Using these, the Israelis built a full-scale mock-up of the terminal at their Ophira air base. There they rehearsed every facet of the mission over and over again.

Those planning the mission were also aided by information that was being furnished by members of the Israeli secret service. They had slipped into Uganda from Kenya and, disguising themselves as airport workers, were able to find out the number of terrorists involved in the operation and what kinds of weapons they had. They also learned that Idi Amin had sent a special plane to nearby Somalia to bring in more terrorists to be used in guarding the hostages.

The rescue mission was code-named "Thunderbolt." On July 3, six days after the hijacking, four C-130 Hercules transports took off from Ophira and flew south at a low altitude to avoid radar detection, heading over the Red Sea and Ethiopia. Above the four planes flew a Boeing 707 that had been turned into an aerial command post with sophisticated communications equipment. And high above the command plane flew deadly F-4 Phantom jet fighters. Their job was to protect the transports in case any hostile country tried to intercept them.

During the flight, the Boeing 707 radioed ahead to the control tower at Entebbe to announce that President Amin was coming in to land and requesting that the runway lights be turned on. One of the C-130s carried an exact copy of Amin's black Mercedes. If their scheme worked, the Israelis planned to load the car with commandos and race to the old terminal before the terrorists and the Ugandans realized what was going on.

The other Israeli transports carried commandos whose job it would be to secure the airfield and the control tower. They also were assigned to put out of action several Ugandan

Mig-7 fighter planes, which could shoot down the Israeli transports as they began their return trip.

At the end of their 2,620-mile flight from Ophira, the four transports came in low over Lake Victoria. The pilots grinned when they saw the runway lights had been turned on for the "presidential visit." One of the transports dropped flares and explosives at the far end of the runway to distract and frighten the Ugandan troops who were guarding the airfield. Meanwhile, the other three C-130s touched down and taxied to a stop. Within seconds, the airport was alive with Israeli commandos.

The black Mercedes rolled down a ramp and sped for the old terminal. But a pair of sentries in front of the building noticed the car was not carrying their president but was filled instead with gun-bearing commandos, so they opened fire. The Israelis fired back. One of the sentries was killed instantly. The other ran screaming toward the control tower before he, too, was shot.

The commandos stormed into the terminal building, shouting in Hebrew for everyone to lie flat. The two German terrorists were gunned down almost immediately, but the leader of the assault, Lieutenant Colonel Yonatan Netanyahu, was also killed, along with three other commandos. Three of the hostages (who stood up instead of lying down) were fatally shot, too.

Within less than an hour after the commandos had arrived, the transports were back in the air with the freed hostages aboard. The aircraft made a refueling stop at the Nairobi airport in Kenya, where doctors treated the wounded. Four hours later, the terrible drama ended when the planes landed at Tel Aviv's Ben Gurion Airport. Most of the freed men and women were so overcome by emotion they could not speak.

The spectacular rescue of the hijacked passengers at the Entebbe airport served as a clear-cut demonstration of how a highly skilled, specially trained force can achieve concrete results in the war against terrorism. "I'm proud of what we did

and happy that we have an army, and units and officers like
these," said Israeli Defense Minister Shimon Peres. "But I hope
we never have to repeat it."

Israel officially came into existence on May 14, 1948, and
the following day Arab armies from Egypt, Lebanon, Syria,
Jordan, and Iraq attacked the new nation. The Israeli Defense
Forces (IDF) took shape during the war, which ended early in

1949 with an Israeli victory. The IDF has been at war almost continually ever since, making it the most combat experienced fighting force in the world.

At first, the IDF opposed the idea of special forces. Everyone was to go by the book; nobody was to be "special." But during the frequent border clashes between Arab and Israeli troops in the early 1950s, elite units were developed as a response to Arab infiltrators.

As the IDF grew, so did its Special Forces. When the second Arab-Israeli war erupted in late 1956, Israeli Special Forces Units played a critical role. A newly formed parachute brigade made a historic combat jump at the Mitla Pass to lead Israeli forces to victory in the Sinai Peninsula.

In the years that followed, Israel's Special Forces took on a legendary status. In the 1967 Six-Day War, in which Israel defeated Egypt, Jordan, and Syria, an IDF parachute brigade captured the city of Jerusalem. Countless commando raids against PLO bases in neighboring Arab countries were a feature of the 1967–1970 War of Attrition.

During Operation Peace for Galilee in 1982, in which a large force of Israeli troops attacked southern and central Lebanon in response to attacks by the Palestine Liberation Organization (PLO), an elite Israeli commando unit was assigned to storm the 12th-century Beaufort Castle, built atop a 1,500-foot-high granite mountain. From the mountaintop, the Palestinians had been firing artillery and mortar shells into northern Israel.

The commandos started up the mountain under the cover of darkness. The Palestinians fired at them from caves and behind rocks. Then the commandos called for an artillery barrage to blast the guerrillas' hiding places. Part of the castle was destroyed in the bombardment. As soon as the artillery fire ceased, the commandos charged the castle behind a barrage of fire from their Uzi submachine guns. Within minutes, the castle was in Israeli hands.

Israeli commandos can, seemingly, handle any assignment, small or large. In 1994, Israeli commandos in a pair of

helicopter gunships swept into a small village deep in Lebanon and kidnapped a Muslim guerrilla from his home and brought him back to Israel for questioning. Once at the site, the commandos wrapped up the job in seven minutes.

Most of Israel's Special Forces Units are drawn from the parachute corps. Volunteers undergo two months of basic training that stresses long forced marches over rough terrain to toughen the recruits and build their endurance. Three months of specialist training follows. During this time, each recruit learns a particular skill, anything from driver to medic, from machine gunner to demolitions expert.

Mine-sweeping Israeli tanks clear the road north of Beaufort Castle after Israelis captured the Palestinian stronghold. (U.S. Navy)

The recruits also get intensive weapons training. The 9-mm Uzi submachine gun is the commandos' favorite weapon. Named after its designer, Uziel Galil, it features a 25- or 30-round magazine that is inserted through the pistol grip, making the weapon a cinch to reload. One can even reload in the dark. The weapon has sand and dust grooves that are meant to collect any dust that might enter and jam the firing mechanism. The Uzi weighs only nine pounds, can fire 600 rounds a minute, and has a range of about 100 yards. Used by many Special Forces units around the world, it is even carried by the Secret Service agents who guard U.S. presidents.

IDF Special Forces recruits also practice assaults using helicopters and armored personnel carriers. The final month of training is given over to learning parachuting techniques.

After completing their training and receiving their wings, recruits are assigned to one of the IDF's Special Forces groups. There is a wide range of units from which to choose, each designated Sayeret (reconnaissance). Sayeret Shaldeg is an infiltration and sabotage unit. Members of Sayeret Carob are trained for mountain warfare. Sayeret Orev is a reconnaissance unit that also carries out antitank assignments. Sayeret Tzanhim is a rapid-assault unit. Sayeret Almond specializes in patrols deep into the desert. After the spectacular raid on Entebbe, the Israelis formed a new unit to specialize in hostage rescues. Active today, it is known as Unit 269.

The Middle East abounds with antiterrorist forces. Egypt boasts a Marine assault brigade, two air assault brigades, and two parachute brigades. Jordan maintains three 500-man parachute units specially trained in guerrilla fighting. Syria has three commando battalions, which were in action in Lebanon almost constantly during the late 1980s. But in evaluating Special Forces in the Middle East, it is generally agreed that Israel's are Number 1 and that those of no other nation come even close.

Special Forces–
Related
Abbreviations
and Acronyms

A-Team	Unit of 12 Special Forces soldiers
ARSOF	Army Special Operations Forces
ARVN	Army of the Republic of Vietnam
ATC	Air Transport Command
AWACS	Airborne Warning and Control System
BUD/S	Basic Underwater Demolition/SEAL
CADS	Controlled Aerial Delivery System
CIA	Central Intelligence Agency
CO	Commanding Officer
CRW	Counterrevolutionary Warfare
DIA	Defense Intelligence Agency
DoD	Department of Defense
ECM	Electronic Countermeasures
ELINT	Electronic Intelligence
EW	Electronic Warfare
FLIR	Forward-Looking Infrared Radar
GIGN	Gendarmerie Nationale
GPS	Global Positioning System
GSG9	Grenzschutzgruppe 9

HAHO	High-Altitude, High-Opening
HALO	High-Altitude, Low-Opening
ICBM	Intercontinental Ballistic Missile
IDF	Israeli Defense Forces
IR	Infrared
IRA	Irish Republican Army
JCS	Joint Chiefs of Staff
NASA	National Aeronautics and Space Administration
NATO	North Atlantic Treaty Organization
OSS	Office of Strategic Services (the forerunner of the CIA)
PDF	Panamanian Defense Forces
PGM	Precision-Guided Munitions (also called "smart bombs")
PLO	Palestine Liberation Organization
RAF	Royal Air Force (the military air arm of the United Kingdom)
RCAF	Royal Canadian Air Force
RPG	Rocket-Propelled Grenade
SAC	Strategic Air Command
SAM	Surface-to-Air Missile
SAS	Special Air Service
SBS	Special Boat Squadron
SBU	Special Boat Unit
SCUBA	Self-Contained Underwater Breathing Apparatus
SDV	SEAL Delivery Vehicle
SEAL	*SE*a *A*ir *L*and commandos
SMG	Submachine gun
SOF	Special Operations Forces
SOT	Special Operations Training
STAR	Surface-to-Air Recovery system
STOL	Short Takeoff and Landing

TOW	Tube-launched, optically-tracked, wire-guided missile
UDT	Underwater Demolition Team
USAF	United States Air Force
USSOCOM	U.S. Special Operations Command
VC	Vietcong

For Additional Reading

Adams, James. *Secret Armies*. New York: Atlantic Monthly Press, 1987.

Bank, Aaron. *From OSS to Green Berets*. Novato, Calif.: Presidio Press, 1986.

Beckwith, Colonel Charlie L., and Donald Knox. *Delta Force: The Army's Elite Counter-Terrorist Unit*. New York: Harcourt, Brace, Jovanovich, 1983.

Debay, Yves. *The French Foreign Legion in Action*. London: Windrow & Greene, 1992.

Dockery, Kevin. *Seals in Action*. New York: Avon Books, 1991.

Eshel, David. *Elite Fighting Units*. London: Arms and Armour Press, 1984.

Griswold, Terry, and D. M. Giangreco. *Delta, America's Elite Counter-Terrorist Force*. Osceola, Wisc.: Motorbooks International, 1992.

Halberstadt, Hans. *Green Berets: Unconventional Warriors*. Novato, Calif.: Presidio Press, 1988.

Landau, Alan M., and Frieda W. Landau. *Airborne Rangers*. Osceola, Wisc.: Motorbooks International, 1992.

Lucas, James. *Hitler's Mountain Troops*. London: Arms and Armour Press, 1992.

Moyer, Frank A. *Special Forces Foreign Weapons Handbook*. Boulder, Colo.: Paladin Press, 1983.

Nadel, Joel, with J. R. Wright. *Special Men and Special Missions*. London: Greenhill Books, 1994.

Rottman, Gordon, *World Special Forces Insignia*. London: Osprey Publishing, 1989.

Simpson, Charles M. *Inside the Green Berets*. New York: Berkley Books, 1984.

Waller, Douglas C. *The Commandos: The Inside Story of America's Secret Soldiers*. New York: Simon & Schuster, 1994.

Watson, James, and Kevin Dockery. *Point Man*. New York: William Morrow, 1993.

Index

Italic page numbers indicate illustrations.

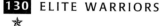